COLLEEN CARPENTER CULLINAN

REDEEMING
THE STORY

Women, Suffering, and Christ

continuum

NEW YORK • LONDON

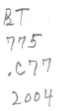

Copyright © 2004 by Colleen Carpenter Cullinan

The Continuum International Publishing Group
15 East 26th Street, New York, NY 10010

The Continuum International Publishing Group Ltd
The Tower Building, 11 York Road, London SE1 7NX

Unless otherwise indicated, biblical quotations are from the New Revised Standard Version Bible, copyright 1989, Division of Christian Education of the National Council of the Churches of Christ in the United States of America. Used by permission. All rights reserved.

COVER ART: Diana Ong, Blue Lady #1/SuperStock

COVER DESIGN: Corey Kent

Library of Congress Cataloging-in-Publication Data

Cullinan, Colleen Carpenter.
  Redeeming the story : women, suffering, and Christ / Colleen Carpenter Cullinan.
    p.   cm.
  Includes index.
  ISBN 0-8264-1610-1 (pbk.)
  1. Redemption—Christianity. 2. Narrative theology. 3. Feminist theology. I. Title.
BT775.C77 2004
234'.3—dc22

                              2004006694

Printed in the United States of America

04 05 06 07 08 09   10 9 8 7 6 5 4 3 2 1

To my mother,
Donna Bee Loess Carpenter
1942–1988

—ɷ—

Your love is always with me

CONTENTS

ACKNOWLEDGMENTS

This book grew out of my dissertation, and so I'd like to thank my disscrtation committee first. Professors Anthony Yu, Anne Carr, and Kathryn Tanner both supported and continually challenged me as I wrote. I benefited from their enthusiastic approval and from their direct criticisms; I am honored to have worked with each of them, and am grateful for all they taught me. I would also like to thank the Louisville Institute, which funded a year of my dissertation work. One chapter of the dissertation has already made its way out into the world: A previous version of "A Maternal Discourse of Redemption: Speech and Suffering in Morrison's *Beloved*" originally appeared in *Religion & Literature*, Volume 34, Issue 2 (Summer 2002). Reprint permission is granted by the University of Notre Dame English Department.

I have been repeatedly and pleasantly surprised over the years to discover that wherever I go, the dynamic, powerful, amazing, faith-filled, and lovely spiritual home that I leave behind is not the last one I'll ever know. Moreover, my faith has been enriched and deepened by the challenges each new place has offered me. I learned to sing at my childhood parish, St. Raphael's Catholic Church in Naperville, Illinois, and song has been central to my experience of worship ever since. I joined the choir the second I arrived at the Harvard-Radcliffe Catholic Student Center, and it was that community that introduced me to feminism and justice as key issues in the practice of our faith. It wasn't until I spent a year in the company of the Sinsinawa Dominicans in Chicago, however, that I saw and truly believed that compassion was the most powerful force in the universe—and that it is and must be the driving force behind all work for justice, peace, and new life. Sisters Erica Jordan, Judy Seiberlich, Lisa Williams, Margaret McGuirk, Rose Conway, Jane Schollmeyer, and Jeri Cashman were my companions, friends, and mothers during my year of volunteer work with them. In Minneapolis, I was privileged to sing under the directorship of Tom Conry at the Newman Center at the University of Minnesota. His music rings with passion, compassion, hope, and faith, and when I sang in his choir, I knew I was praying twice. I would like to thank him for writing "What God Has Now Begun," the song that anchors this book, and am deeply appreciative to him and to Oregon Catholic Press for letting me reprint some of the lyrics. I also need to thank Esther Broner for her kindness in responding to the queries of a random graduate student in cyberspace; Abingdon Press for their permission to use an excerpt from Roberta Bondi's powerful memoir, *Memories of God*; International Creative Management for permission to quote from Toni Morrison's novel, *Beloved*; and HarperCollins and Frances Goldin Literary Agency, Inc. for permission to use excerpts from Barbara Kingsolver's *Animal Dreams*. The creative voices on which my analysis and commentary rest are breathtakingly beautiful, not to mention revolutionary in their visions of the truth of our world. God bless the artists.

Here in Montevideo, I am blessed to be part of several faith communities. The first is of course my parish, St. Joseph's, which is now part of a larger Area Parish Community named The River of Life. My family has also been enriched by worship and Sunday school at the United Methodist Church, where my son Thomas has been learning the songs and coloring the pictures and hearing the stories, over and over again, that will be the foundation of his Christian faith. I was invited by a group of marvelous women to join their Bible study, and as the only one in the group with young children instead of young grandchildren, I am humbled by their wisdom, grace, and wealth of experience. I offer thanks to each of them—Janis Oakes, Sally Haugen, Lois Hein, Karen Vaske, Jackie Herfurth, and Mary Spain—whose patient attention to the presence of Christ in their lives is a joy to see and a model for me to emulate. I also need to thank Patrick Moore, whose faith challenges my own, whose passion and commitment enriches our entire community, and whose coffee shop, Java River, serves up the absolute best in locally-grown food, local art and music, and imported organic chocolate (without which this book would never have been completed). Finally, there is the group that has never managed to name itself, a gathering of organic farmers, artists, community organizers, and activists who recognize the Spirit that grounds all they do. Our "Quaker-ish" meeting includes Audrey Arner and Richard Handeen, Mike Jacobs and Malena Handeen, Marilyn Handeen, Kay and Annette Fernholz, Lucy and Gene Tokheim, Amy Bacigalupo and Paul Wymar, and Dorothy Anderson. The time I spent in silence with them, listening for our breath and the breath of God, made a long dark winter endurable; the time we spent sharing dinner, chasing children, and singing made hope possible. I cannot thank them enough.

I also need to thank Henry Carrigan, my editor, who not only remembered the first public paper I ever gave, but who believed in this project enough to shepherd it to completion. Amy Wagner, the senior managing editor with whom I worked, responded quickly and patiently to my numerous emails, full of questions and problems that she invariably resolved. I am deeply grateful to them both.

Finally, I would like to thank my family. I began this project before I was a mother, and I now have two lovely sons, Thomas and Patrick. I would like to thank both of them for changing my life completely, and for being my best teachers in the always-difficult fields of love, patience, and kindness. With luck I will return the favor by educating them in *my* chosen field, theology, where it appears they need a lot of work. Having seen a few too many *Veggie Tales* videos, Thomas is convinced that God is a cucumber. Patrick isn't talking yet, but I have more hope for his theological development, as he insists on holding hands and saying grace at least five or six times during each meal. My husband Brendon—physician, photographer, woodworker, artist—survived my long years of graduate school with grace and good humor, and is unfailing in his support and love. I am honored to be sharing my life with such a wonderful man, and I am endlessly grateful for the love and care with which he fills our home.

I dedicated this book to my mother, Donna Carpenter, whose life was too short and too filled with pain. Despite her struggles, she filled my life and the lives of my brother and sister with a tenacious, passionate love that shaped us and will never let us go. I know she's proud of me, and that she'd be thrilled about this book. I love you, Mom.

INTRODUCTION
Converting the Imagination

When we set out on our wayfare, we feared death had claimed his own,
And we wondered in that darkness who would roll away the stone.
Now the tomb itself lies open where the linen shroud was spread,
And our God has raised our brother, made him first-born of the dead.
So the light has been enkindled, and the morning makes us one;
Then let all the earth set seal to what God has now begun.

Ancient Death is yet within us and his power continues still:
Yet he walks no more unbounded, and pray God, no longer will.
As the one who raised the dead has now become the one who died,
Now the ending of our story only people may decide.
Death has gathered us together, and the dying makes us one;
Then let all the earth set seal to what God has now begun.[1]

At the heart of Christianity is the promise of redemption: the promise that, through Jesus Christ, we can find wholeness, reconciliation with God, forgiveness, love—everything that God ever meant for us to have and to be, before God's creation was so cruelly deformed by sin and suffering. It is an enormous promise, a staggeringly tremendous offer of hope. It is almost too good to be true—and yet Christians embrace it as the central Truth on which their world is built. As a Christian, I am one of those who recognizes this promise as the center of what is real and true in my life, and yet I also know that there are at least two deeply troubling problems that prevent others from embracing Christian teaching about redemption. The first problem is one that Christians have struggled with for a long time, and that struggle can be seen in Tom Conry's powerful Easter hymn "What God Has Now Begun." Here the congregation sings with the voice of the first Christian community, believing at first that death had conquered Christ, and learning in surprise and wonder that, instead, God has conquered death. Yet the beginning of the second verse reminds us force-fully that this story is not over: no one lived happily ever after, for "ancient death is yet within us, and his power continues still." Death has been con-quered, but death is not dead. Suffering is still very real; death is still very powerful. Those of us who place our hope in the redemption offered by Jesus have to face this problem: if redemption is real, and finished-and-done in the death of Jesus, then how do we explain the suffering that still exists in the world?

In contrast to this ancient and acknowledged problem, the second problem seems "new"—at least, few people had discussed it, or even noticed it, until recently. Yet in some ways, the second problem with redemption is the more troubling: what about women? Over the past two thousand years, the great promise of redemption has too often been framed in ways that have persistently and systematically hurt women. The story of redemption was often told in such a way that women were iden-tified as the source of sin and death in God's once-perfect world: "You are the devil's gateway," one of the earliest Church Fathers told women. "How easily you destroyed man, the image of God. Because of the death which you brought upon us, even the Son of God had to die."[2] More than that, some aspects of Christian tradition insisted that women's nature was so corrupt that not even the redemption offered by Jesus was enough to transform it. Even St. Paul seemed to believe this: he argues in the first let-ter to Timothy that redemption comes through Christ, but women will be saved through childbearing (1 Timothy 2:15). This odd claim, that women aren't "really" saved, or are "more" guilty, or still "need" to be punished, is a disturbing theme in Christian history. In fact, this insistence that there is something different about women—something wrong with them—has fundamentally shaped our understanding of redemption, with dire conse-quences for women (and men, and our understanding of God).

We need to reimagine redemption in a way that addresses the two problems I have described. We need to speak of Jesus and the promise of redemption in a way that women (and all those who suffer) will recognize as redemptive, and embrace with hope and joy. I believe that the first step toward that goal is *listening to the voices of women* as they speak of God, Jesus, suffering, healing, transformation, sin, and hope. But I have also become convinced that, in the end, a credible theological message is not enough. Ultimately, even the "right" theology can't solve these problems. That is because the problem is less with the *theology* than with the *story*. Women's imaginations—and men's, too—are held in thrall by the story we traditionally tell about Jesus: the story of an angry Father God who desires the death of his beloved Son in order that sinful humans can be forgiven for their sins and not sent, as they deserve to be, to a fiery hell forever. That story has as its centerpiece the brutal crucifixion, which is presented as not only necessary but desired by God *in his goodness*, a paradox that can only poison our understanding of goodness, love, justice, and mercy. Critiquing this story is not enough; theologizing in a new direction is not enough. To break the hold this story has on the Christian imagination, we need to address the imagination itself, and we can only do this in ways that fully engage the imagination: that is, this is a problem that can only be solved with a new story.

Only a story can replace a story: a rational argument and a logical theory may make sense, but they won't transform our hearts and lives. New "images" of God that don't fit into the old stories have no anchor, no hold on our hearts. They exist in the rational corner of our minds but not in the worshipping center of our existence, the core of our being where we meet God. That core has been shaped by a lifetime of story, song, and symbol, and if we rationally wish to change it, then we must seek out new stories, new songs, and new symbols. The story we know of sacrifice, anger, and sin needs to be replaced by other stories—stories of love, forgiveness, and renewal, stories like the ones Jesus told. Unfortunately, while theology can point us to the need for those stories, it cannot write them.

And so the heart of this book focuses on stories: stories told by women today, and stories by and about Jesus. We need both to help us make sense of the Christian promise of redemption. By listening to women's voices speaking of suffering and healing, brokenness and wholeness, death and new life, I believe that we can find new ways to understand the paradoxical idea of redemption. And by listening again to the Gospel stories of Jesus—with our eyes and ears newly opened to women's concerns and insights—we will discover a new way to understand the story of Jesus' life, death, and resurrection: the story of our redemption.

We also need to face the fact that stories, however powerful, can be rejected, or worse, misinterpreted. After all, Jesus told stories, and we have fairly persistently ignored or reshaped them in order to avoid their challenge. For example, the story of the Prodigal Son envisions a father (God?) who is not interested in or concerned with sin, but longs only for joyful reunion with his lost son. As a thought experiment, theologian Robin Collins once retold that story in such a way that, when the younger son begs forgiveness, he does not receive it. Instead, the father tells him that he cannot return to the family until his debt is repaid. Knowing that he will never be able to pay it, the younger son despairs—until his older brother steps in and offers to pay what his brother owes. The older brother goes out to the fields, and works until he drops dead of exhaustion, at which point the father proclaims the debt forgiven, and welcomes the younger son into the house. This is a complete reversal of the story as we know it, and yet, Collins points out, it is a frighteningly accurate account of the story through which many of us understand redemption.[3]

Given our reluctance to attend properly to even the powerful stories Jesus told, I believe that the ultimate problem we face is a failure of imagination, which is born of a failure of belief in both God and ourselves. We cannot imagine God's great love; we cannot imagine that God loves people like us. We are too convinced, as the medieval mystic Julian of Norwich pointed out, of our own shame and faults.[4] We have been blinded by sin so greatly that we do not understand that we are beloved. Redemption calls us to live as God's beloved children, and to understand our lives as part of the ongoing love story between God and creation. Jesus' love, Jesus' presence, and Jesus' stories all push us toward living in God's story of redemption and hope. While a few of us, in some places and at some times, have heard the message and let it transform our lives, for the most part we prefer to continue to believe in our need for punishment, our essential badness. Nevertheless, stories, songs, and other artistic creations are our best hope for healing our broken imaginations. Jesus, after all, envisioned a world turned upside down in his stories, and we need to keep telling them. More than that, we need to find people who can tell the story of the life, death, and resurrection of Jesus *as he might have told it*, in a startling, upside-down, surprising way, one that rejects all forms of judgmental violence and instead reveals the unfathomable depths of love and laughter at the heart of God.

Notes

1. Tom Conry, "What God Has Now Begun," on *The Fire Within the Night*, compact disc (Portland, OR: OCP Publications, 1994). © 1989 Team Publications. Published by OCP Publications, 5536 Ne Hassalo, Portland, OR 97213. All rights reserved. Used with permission.

2. Tertullian, quoted in Mary Daly, *Beyond God the Father: Toward a Philosophy of Women's Liberation, with an Original Reintroduction by the Author* (Boston: Beacon Press, 1985; originally published 1973), 44.

3. Robin Collins, "Understanding Atonement: A New and Orthodox Theory" (speech, annual meeting of the American Academy of Religion, Philadelphia, Pennsylvania, 1995).

4. Jane McAvoy, *The Satisfied Life: Medieval Women Mystics on Atonement* (Cleveland, OH: The Pilgrim Press, 2000), 18.

Chapter 1

TELLING THE WRONG STORY

There was a woman who had been suffering from hemorrhages for twelve years. She had endured much under many physicians, and had spent all that she had; and she was no better, but rather grew worse. She had heard about Jesus, and came up behind him in the crowd and touched his cloak, for she said, "If I but touch his clothes, I will be made well." Immediately her hemorrhage stopped; and she felt in her body that she was healed of her disease. Immediately aware that power had gone forth from him, Jesus turned about in the crowd and said, "Who touched my clothes?" And his disciples said to him, "You see the crowd pressing in on you; how can you say, 'Who touched me?'" He looked all around to see who had done it. But the woman, knowing what had happened to her, came in fear and trembling, fell down before him, and told him the whole truth. He said to her, "Daughter, your faith has made you well; go in peace, and be healed of your disease." (Mark 5:25–34)

The story of the woman with the hemorrhage is a powerful story of healing and redemption. Suffering touched every part of this woman's life. She was poor; she had spent all she had. She was in pain, suffering greatly at the hands of many doctors. She was an outcast in society, made unclean by a constant flow of polluting blood. And finally, she was a woman, which was not only the source of her illness, but made all the other problems worse. All of these concrete, physical problems led to terrible emotional and spiritual suffering, too: since she was unclean, she felt shame before others and knew that she was unworthy before God. And just as suffering had touched every part of her life, so, too, did Jesus' healing.

When her flow of blood dried up, her life was transformed. It was not just her body that was healed, it was her *life*. She was able to "go in peace" in a way previously unimaginable to her: she was freed from her illness, her shame, her loneliness, and her fear. She, like others whom Jesus healed, was suddenly able to praise God, to testify to the saving power of Jesus, to follow Jesus. She had been saved.

The story we tell about this woman tells us not only about her, but about Jesus, and about the God that Jesus called Abba. We can learn a lot about women, redemption, and Jesus by paying attention to this story; but first we need to think about why storytelling is important, and why it's important not only to get the facts right (we're good at that, we pay attention to facts in our society), but to get the *story* right. A story is more than "just the facts, ma'am." A story is an *interpretation* of the facts. A story links isolated facts together with causes and motivations and perhaps even with other facts that we thought were unrelated, and suddenly we are able to see *as a whole* something that unfolded in pieces, over time. Telling the wrong story, then—even with the right facts—is perhaps worse than simply getting the facts wrong. Because if you don't understand the causes, or how the facts fit together, or if your story pulls together facts that really should stay separate, or leaves out crucial facts, if any or all of that happens, then whatever was true about what you started with can end up as the worst sort of lie.

Human beings tell stories all the time. We are storytellers by nature: we are fascinated by the power of stories, by the way they entertain, teach, introduce new ideas, and explore difficult problems. We use stories to illustrate our arguments, to explain difficult concepts, to pass on family history, and ultimately, to make sense of our lives. We live in time, and the only way to make sense of things over time is by connecting them together into a story. The enormous power of storytelling is the power to make order out of chaos: we start with the facts—isolated events—and we weave them together into a coherent, narrative whole. However, the enormous problem with storytelling is that far too often, even if we get the facts right, the story we create goes terribly wrong. You can see this with children: listen to them as they try to make sense of the world. Often their interpretations of what's happening around them are wildly off (or too true to bear, which is another issue entirely). For example, a few years ago my three-year-old son and I were returning from a vacation, and our plane landed late at night. Thomas was exhausted and fell asleep on the luggage cart as I hauled it to the shuttle stop, where we took a bus to our car. When the bus dropped us off, I was carrying a sleeping boy, and facing a pile of luggage and a car seat that I needed to install in the back seat. Since I couldn't put Thomas in the back until I had his car seat buckled in, I put him in the front, in the driver's seat. Then I climbed in the back and started to wrestle with his car seat. He woke up and immediately started to cry. "No, Mommy, no!" he sobbed. "I too small to drive! I too small to drive!"

Poor Thomas! He looked at the situation—sitting in the driver's seat, Mom in the back, a long drive home ahead—and constructed a fairly reasonable interpretation of what was happening. The only problem was, he was completely wrong. Unfortunately, a lot of us do the same thing more often than we know, and the most common place we do it is in our understanding of religion. Faith is, after all, not an easy thing to explain, nor understand. It often involves paradox, mystery, and things that don't really make rational sense, even if they do make our hearts burn within us. This is the ideal place for a story to help us make sense of things and the ideal place for a story to lead us completely astray. And I believe that we have gone terribly astray, that we persistently tell ourselves and each other the wrong stories about Jesus and about Christianity.

Oh, we have the facts right: God became human and lived and died among us, then rose to new life. The problem lies in how we interpret these facts, how we transform them from isolated events into a story that makes sense, touches our hearts, and is true. We need to understand the causes (Did our sins lead to the death of Jesus?), the motivations (Did God want Jesus to die? Is perfect obedience the best way to understand why Jesus did the things he did?), the key moments of the story (Is the most important part the death of Jesus? Or is it the resurrection? Or maybe the incarnation?), and how everything fits together. I have come to believe that the wrong story about Jesus is a story about sin, punishment, blood, and death, and we tell it all the time, even if we think we believe a story about love, forgiveness, grace, and mercy. In her fascinating memoir *Memories of God*, Roberta Bondi explains how she realized that her faith was rooted in the wrong story of Jesus. Since Bondi is a theologian and scholar of early Christian history, she knew and understood what the church believes about Christ, his crucifixion, and redemptive activity much better than most of us ever will. Committed in her faith and practice to a loving and forgiving God, she dreamt one night of the God who lived in her heart, even though her head knew better:

> I dreamed I was with [my husband] Richard in my great-aunt Blacky's farmhouse on the hill outside Morganfield, Kentucky. It was the middle of a good-smelling early summer day, with the insects humming and the hassock fan whirring on the front porch. Sunlight poured through the kitchen into the back hall where I stood, but I was in darkness. I was sobbing and

wringing my hands outside her green-tiled bathroom. In the bathroom Richard was kneeling in the bathtub, his neck held over the drain by a powerful looking, dark-haired man with a huge knife I knew had come to kill me. "Don't hurt her," Richard was saying. "Take me; just don't hurt her; take me."

In my dream I was dying with grief. I wanted to shout, "No, no; I'm here, leave Richard alone," but I couldn't make any sound. As I watched in horror, the killer slit Richard's throat and red blood flowed all over the green tiles.

Then the dream was over, and I began to rise out of sleep, shivering, sobbing, and covered with sweat . . . In the very same instant the words formed in my mind, "this is what you've always thought the crucifixion is about, but this is not it" . . .

But what on earth had I believed? In spite of myself, since childhood I had always known that I had thought of the work of Christ in terms of sacrifice for sin, but had this meant to me that the crucifixion of Jesus was like the terrible murder in my place of Richard in Aunt Blacky's green bathroom? Did I believe my sin was the cause of Jesus' murder, and if so, what did I think my sin was? Did I believe that, all things being equal, God would have preferred that I be murdered instead? Who was Jesus in all this, and how did he participate? Who did I think it was who had chosen that murder as a remedy for sin? Was it Jesus? Was it God or the devil, or were they the same person? What awful thing was my dream telling me I had been thinking about God?[1]

Bondi's search, through prayer and the cultivation of childhood memory, for what she believed and why, revealed a faith formed in early experiences and in powerful stories. It took years of prayer, new experiences, and new stories for Bondi to renew and rebuild her faith in God, her understanding of how love works, and her beliefs about how the world is put together. This book is meant to be an aid for those who wish to embark on a similar journey. Journeys are, of course, adventure stories: we abandon the old and familiar, and go forth to struggle in the wilderness. Sometimes we get lost, sometimes we are hungry, often we wish we could give up and go back, until at long last, we find ourselves—changed forever—at home, somewhere new. For our purposes, we are about to abandon the old, familiar (but terribly flawed) stories about Jesus, and strike out toward a new home deep in the heart of God. Our own imaginations will be working against us—the stories we have always believed, the patterns that make sense to us, the stock characters that "should" act in certain ways. Yet imaginations, like bodies, can be healed; like the woman with the hemorrhage, we will reach out for new life.

The key to our journey will be trying to understand both the idea and the story of redemption in a new way. Our familiar ideas about redemption are in fact deeply flawed, mostly because we tend to associate redemption only with sin, and neglect the other ways in which we are separated from God. Suffering is one of the most terrible ways we are separated from God; indeed, intense suffering can separate us from everything except the excruciating knowledge of pain. Physical suffering is a terrible, overwhelming reality for much of the world and that reality is almost entirely ignored when we speak of redemption in conventional ways. Human *bodies* need to be redeemed as part of the project of redeeming human beings, for we are not just spirits "trapped" in bodies, but creatures who exist as the marvelous and miraculous combination of the dust of the earth and the breath of God. Recognizing this profound truth about the complexity of human beings, Jesus paid attention to people's bodies. He set about feeding the hungry and curing the sick wherever he went. At times, he did not seem to truly distinguish between forgiveness and healing, offering both when only one was requested. He knew that those who were hungry or in pain needed redemption in its widest and most inclusive sense—they needed redemption as liberation from the chains of sickness, as wholeness in body and spirit—and he offered just this kind of redemption by healing bodies as he forgave sins. Today, the church offers redemption from sin, and reminds us that we suffer in punishment for our sins. This is a hollow redemption. It ignores our bodies, and pretends that the wholeness we seek is a matter of belief (in God and Christ) and attitude (repentance, obedience, humility) instead of a matter of every part of our being: physical, mental, social, and spiritual. Asian theologian C. S. Song, whose understanding of Christianity has been profoundly shaped by the poverty and hunger that mark so much of Asia, argues that redemption is nothing less than "a question of life and death, the question of whether love is rich enough to fill an empty stomach, strong enough to restore a disfigured humanity, and powerful enough to create life in the midst of death."[2] Dare we believe that the love of Jesus is that rich, that strong, that powerful? Or shall we just stick with the familiar: the forgiveness of sins?

The biblical promise of redemption is not as limited as we have come to believe. Instead, it is God's promise to renew all of creation: all things past and present, all people dead and living, all of creation, in all of time. Like the woman with the hemorrhage, we seek much more than the forgiveness of our sins. Like her, too, we must be willing to reach out and grasp that which will heal us. The story we tell about redemption must reflect these realities—this understanding of God and God's promise, of ourselves and what we can and must do, and of suffering in the world. The nature of God, of humanity, and of the world—a particular understanding of these three things will be displayed in our story of redemption, as in every other story. Further, every story of redemption is rooted in a particular *relationship* between the self, God, and the world. Each of these three elements is dependent on the others: change your understanding of even one, and the whole story changes. One of the biggest issues we need to face, as we construct our new story of redemption, is the fact that traditional theology has left us with only a partial understanding of the self, God, and the world. Over the past two thousand years, the great majority of theologians have focused on men's experiences of themselves as sons, fathers, and brothers; men's experiences of God, and men's experiences of how the world works. Until very recently, the ideas, insights, and feelings of women have been ignored and dismissed. In the next several chapters, we will be looking carefully at how women understand themselves, God, and the world, in order to gain new perspectives on how the story of redemption might be told in a different way. Once we have looked at the stories women tell about redemption, our journey will take us back to Jesus, and the stories we tell about him in the Gospels. Jesus loved telling stories—parables—that revealed the world in new and surprising ways, and some theologians have even described Jesus as a parable of God. That's a powerful way of describing Jesus: a story told by God about the truth of the world, revealing it to be unlike anything we might expect, overturning our assumptions and asking us to see everything anew. Jesus is the story God tells us about love and hope, about the poor, the suffering, and the powerless, and about the true place of violence and coercive power in the world. Before any of this, however, we need to have a good sense of our starting point, of what exactly we are leaving behind as we set out. What are the wrong stories that we tell about Jesus? Why exactly are they wrong? What about them is true? What can we save, so we don't start our journey empty-handed?

Traditional Understandings of Redemption

If you ask the average Christian to explain how Jesus saved us, you will most likely hear that Jesus died for our sins. If you push for more detail, the story that comes out runs something like this: God made a perfect world, but Adam and Eve sinned. Their crime was passed down to all of us in the form of "original sin," and now all human beings are sinners, and deserve God's condemnation and punishment. We had no way to escape that punishment, or ever to make ourselves acceptable to God—until Jesus came. Jesus died for us; he took the punishment we deserved. If we believe that, and have faith in the forgiveness God offers us through Jesus, then we are saved. Being saved means that we are now acceptable to God (despite our ongoing sinfulness), and we will go to heaven.

The most important thing to know about this popular account of redemption is that *it is not the only way to understand how Jesus saved us*. In fact, despite the widespread conviction that it is a straightforward account of the ancient teachings of the Christian faith, this is a relatively new story and one that can be seen as a significant departure from earlier traditions. The story I just told is a version of John Calvin's understanding of redemption. Calvin, one of the major figures of the Reformation, wrote in the sixteenth century—1,500 years after the beginnings of Christianity. This is not to say that he's wrong, just that our common understanding of what Christianity is "obviously" about is something that would not have been obvious at all throughout most of Christian history. This is terrific news! It means two very important things for our investigation of redemption. First of all, it means that rejecting today's common assumptions about redemption does not mean rejecting Christianity. After all, if that particular story is not the only way to understand how Jesus saved us, then we can still be Christians even if the story we hold in our hearts is a different one than the one Calvin told. Secondly, it means that there's a possibility that the account of redemption we're looking for is already a part of Christian tradition, or at least, that the building blocks for it exist as a part of tradition. We don't have to "make things up" or work from scratch. Instead, we can seek out elements of past Christian teachings that address suffering and women's experience in ways that make sense to us today. This is, after all, essentially what Calvin did: he did not agree with the stories being told in his lifetime about Jesus and how Jesus saved people, and he searched through Scripture and the Church Fathers and other theologians for something that made more sense to him. Using what he found, he added his own prayerful reflections on the Gospels and his personal experience of the Living Christ, and wrote his story. This is how theology comes to be: it is a combination of tradition and our own experience, and it is always a struggle to find ways to be faithful to both—and to God.

In order to think theologically about redemption, then, we need a solid grounding in the history of Christian teaching about redemption, and we need to ask persistent questions along the way about how any particular teaching does or does not adequately address the experience of women. In other words, we need to examine the *tradition* in light of our *experience*.

Traditional thought about redemption can be divided into two categories: redemption as it is presented in the New Testament, and redemption as later theologians described it. Interestingly enough, the New Testament never really gives us a single, clear understanding of how redemption works. Instead of a straightforward *theory* of redemption, the Gospels and epistles offer us several interesting (and sometimes conflicting) *images* of what redemption is all about. We will examine each of these images in turn, and then we will turn to the theologians, who used the New Testament images as the foundations for their more elaborate theories of redemption. Most of these theories were actually (surprise!) stories, even though they were usually accompanied by formal, logically rigorous arguments exploring every possible implication of the particular story told by the theologian. We will investigate several of the major stories told about redemption, listening especially for how they treat suffering and what they mean for women's lives. In fact, throughout our investigation, I will be referring back to the woman with the hemorrhage. We will attempt to understand these often quite rhetorical explanations of redemption through the eyes of this particular woman, and her very real pain, fear, and need. She will keep us grounded; she will remind us that words and ideas can often hurt us dreadfully—or lead us toward salvation. And so, while examining each story or image of redemption, we will ask: How would this help the woman with the hemorrhage? How might it hurt her? What, in effect, are the consequences of this way of understanding the life, death, and work of Jesus?

This analysis of traditional understandings of redemption is more than just a history lesson. Instead, it serves two important purposes: first, we need to see clearly how the Christian tradition has failed women. Looking over the traditional theories, with the woman with the hemorrhage acting as our guide, will demonstrate in a powerful and precise way that redemption as it has traditionally been understood and interpreted is not, in fact, redemptive for women. Secondly, it is important for us to understand how and where the tradition has supported and given hope to women. The task of rethinking redemption so that it makes sense to women and makes sense of suffering is ultimately a constructive project; it is not about generating a laundry list of complaints about Christianity, nor is it based on the assumption that Christianity has "always" been oppressive and harmful to women. Certainly there have been, and there remain, huge problems, but we cannot forget that there are elements in the tradition that offered hope and healing to the woman with the hemorrhage, and to her sisters, *and to us*. These seeds of hope and promise must be sought out and cultivated as we work toward an understanding of redemption that not only makes sense to women today, but is thoroughly grounded in the living tradition of Christianity.

The New Testament offers us a variety of images that attempt to capture the meaning of redemption: sacrifice, ransom, obedience, the renewal of creation, and resurrection all take their turn at center stage. We need to examine each in turn, and pay attention to the fact that images, just like words, can change in their meaning, depending on the time, place, and people involved. For example, what comes to mind when you hear the word "wilderness"? For many people today, the image is that of a place still pristine and blessedly unaltered by human beings: somewhere to "get away from it all" and perhaps even find the silence of God, away from the craziness of normal life. There is an innocence and even romance associated with the term. This innocence would have been completely foreign to early American settlers, who saw the wilderness around them as the domain of the devil, populated by dangerous savages and desperately in need of conquest by God-fearing Christian people. Our cultural and historical context leads us to very different understandings of a word that "should" translate easily from colonial America of three hundred years ago to today.

Now, given that we will be looking at words, images, and stories about redemption that come from places halfway across the world, from cultures we know nothing about, in times so remote as to be utterly foreign, and that were originally expressed in languages that may or may not translate easily into English, given all that, we need to be very aware that we probably will not have the same reactions or understandings that the original audience did. How big of a problem is that? Actually, it's good to know, to keep at the back of our minds, but ultimately it won't affect the main part of our discussion. Biblical scholars have unearthed a great deal of information about those original understandings, but for the most part I will not be trying to re-create biblical understandings of the idea of ransom, nor medieval notions of honor with respect to the idea of atonement-as-satisfaction. Instead, I am most interested in how a particular image or story will resonate with us today: we are, after all, searching for a way to understand redemption that makes sense to us, not one that made sense to people a long time ago in a place far away. It is perfectly possible for an image or story to be absolutely, fundamentally important to one culture or group of people and absolutely unhelpful to another, not because the *event* captured by the image has changed in importance, but because *the way that event was described* at one time fails to translate to another time or place. In other words, it shouldn't be a big surprise that some of the early images and stories associated with redemption don't sound right to us: we are seeing them through much different cultural lenses, with different assumptions about what's important. If we try to hold onto old images simply because they are old, we can lose sight of what the images were trying to capture in the first place, and we will end up telling the wrong story about redemption. This is, of course, exactly what has happened. Our task, then, is to notice where the images and stories seem to be leading us away from the gracious love of God in Jesus, from the *event* of Jesus' existence with us, and realize that there have to be better ways to describe or capture the truth of that event. We are, in essence, looking for a new translation of the truth about redemption.

One of the most prominent images at the root of our thinking about redemption is that of Jesus' death as *an atoning sacrifice*. This image, while almost overlooked in the Gospels of Matthew, Mark, and Luke, is of great significance for Paul and the writers of some of the later epistles. Interestingly, we tend to assume that the Gospels all talk about the death of Jesus as a sacrifice, and certainly they mention it—among other ideas. For the writers of the synoptic Gospels, however, the idea of sacrifice is not nearly as important as we tend to believe. Here you can see how powerful stories actually hijack other stories: once our imaginations had been captured by Paul's powerful story of sacrifice, we started reading the Gospel accounts of Jesus' life, death, and resurrection with that story, that template, in mind. And we lost the ability to see that the Gospels had other stories to tell.

The image of sacrifice is developed most powerfully in the letter to the Hebrews. In this epistle, a complex portrait is painted of Jesus as both the sacrifice that atones for our sins and as the perfect high priest who offers the sacrifice. Both of these images have roots in everyday Jewish religious life of that era, and so were convincing images at the time, for a particular audience, of how Jesus' death is not only meaningful but of ultimate importance. However, readers of Hebrews today lack the cultural context and often even the historical knowledge we would need to appreciate the profound symbolism and power of passages like this one:

> For if the blood of goats and bulls, with the sprinkling of the ashes of a heifer, sanctifies those who have been defiled so that their flesh is purified, how much more will the blood of Christ, who through the eternal Spirit offered himself without blemish to God, purify our conscience from dead works to worship the living God! (Heb. 9:13–14)

Today we do not think of the blood of goats as purifying; indeed, most of us would rather not think of the blood of goats at all. Being holy, for us, does not have anything to do with animal blood and ashes. If anything, such images lean toward the disgusting and disturbing, and speak to us of religious practices we probably consider "primitive." However, the problem with seeing redemption as a sacrifice is bigger than just this cultural divide. There is also the question of how sacrificial imagery affects our understanding of the suffering of Christ and indeed, of suffering in general. There are two things in particular that concern me about associating redemption with sacrifice: first, we are in danger of sanctifying violence; and second, we are in danger of glorifying suffering.

Sanctifying the violence that tortured and killed Christ means that we see his suffering as holy, as necessary—and as given by God. This has terrible consequences both for our understanding of God and for our ability to respond to suffering, our own or that of others. When we understand redemption as sacrifice, we also understand God as One who demands sacrifice, One who is not satisfied with prayer, repentance, or any form of worship other than the pouring out of blood. This of course goes directly against the prophetic tradition that God demands not sacrifice but justice (for example, see Amos 5:21–24). Moreover, the description of God as someone whose justice demands the death of his own Son is one that, if it applied to a human being, would be recognized instantly as unacceptably violent, punitive, and frightening. Certainly this image does not correspond at all with the loving and merciful Father of whom Jesus himself spoke. In addition, when we tell the (wrong) story of God requiring sacrifice, submission, and acceptance of suffering, we also tell ourselves that to struggle or protest against suffering is sinful. Instead of our liberator, the God who frees us (redeems us), God becomes the source of our suffering. What a grotesque misreading of everything Jesus said and did!

The second problem with understanding redemption as sacrifice is that it tends to glorify suffering. If we see the suffering of Jesus as key to how he saved us, then suffering must be a good thing, at least in this case. It is only a small leap, then—and one made explicitly by many Christians—to the claim that any suffering in our lives is a chance to follow Jesus and be like Jesus in his acceptance and endurance of the agonies of crucifixion. If Jesus' suffering is necessary for salvation, then it is good to share in that suffering, to be humbled by the realization of what Jesus endured for our sake. In this model, there is no place for the idea that suffering is often an evil from which God wishes to save us; Jesus did, after all, heal the sick, not advise them to accept their suffering as a gift from God. Historically, people in power have embraced this model of redemption, and urged the suffering poor to accept their lot as a gift from God. Those who struggle to change the conditions of their lives are then charged with sinful rebellion against God. Again, we have reached a terrible distortion of God's redemptive (healing, renewing) purpose in our lives, made more terrible by the fact that it ends not just in misunderstanding but in *actively preventing* redemptive activity in the world.

Finally, we turn to the woman with the hemorrhage. How does the image of sacrifice help her, or help her understand her situation? I would say that as it has been interpreted in Christian tradition, it cannot truly help and would probably hurt her. For her to know that Jesus' death atones for her sins is something that fails to address all of the truly painful circumstances of her life: her illness, her poverty, and her status as an outcast. Moreover, if we are caught in the trap of believing that suffering is good because it connects us to the redemptive suffering of Jesus, we might even tell her to endure her agony because it was sent to her by God. The woman's struggle against her pain—especially her decision to touch Jesus in order to be healed—could even be seen as sinful presumption. However, Jesus did not see things that way. Instead, he spoke to her kindly and with respect, and he healed her.

The next significant image of redemption that appears in the New Testament is that of Jesus' death serving as a ransom for our sins. Seeing the death of Jesus as the price paid to free us from the grasp of sin and death is an image that is still common today. The idea of ransom calls to mind an image of a captive being set free, and being allowed to return to her rightful home. For us, that home is with God. Being ransomed means that we belong to God again, and sin and death no longer "own" us or have power over us. This is a powerful notion that brilliantly captures both the enslaving character of suffering and the liberating character of God. Without Jesus, we are chained to the evils that afflict us; it is only in Jesus that the chains of our suffering are broken. Not surprisingly, this was one of the favorite images of the early church, and the Eastern Church Fathers developed a fascinating, complex story that enriched and explained it. That atonement theory, known as the "Christus Victor" theory, has its own merits and problems that will be considered later, but for now I would like to address one very intriguing idea associated with this image. "You were bought with a price," Paul assures us (1 Cor. 6:20), that price being the death of Jesus. Interestingly enough, he says this in the context of speaking of our bodies as temples of God: "You were bought with a price; therefore glorify God in your body." His message here is that our bodies, being part of Christ's body, are too precious to abuse. They, too, have been redeemed; they, too, can glorify God. Since we are interested in the redemption of suffering bodies, this suggestion that redemption has something to do with the body—and perhaps even with the presence of God in our bodies—is an important message to remember. Jesus' healing of the woman with the hemorrhage revealed God's compassion and power: it glorified God and it did so through her body. Further, the idea that each of us is valuable enough to "purchase" is an important message for women in a world that all too often reminds them only of their worthlessness.

Another common image, that of redemption through the perfect obedience of Christ, is not nearly as helpful. This image of redemption is expressed most powerfully in Philippians:

> Let the same mind be in you that was in Christ Jesus, who, though he was in the form of God, did not regard equality with God as something to be exploited, but emptied himself, taking the form of a slave, being born in human likeness. And being found in human form, he humbled himself and became obedient to the point of death—even death on a cross. Therefore God also highly exalted him . . . (Phil. 2:5–9)

This emphasis on obedience is a problem in many ways, the most significant of which is that it has led to religious sanction for the subordination and even the abuse of the powerless, and especially of women. In their efforts to imitate Jesus, many Christians saw obedience as the ultimate Christian virtue, and unfortunately came to equate obedience to God with obedience to anyone in a position of authority (in the family, society, or nation). The terrible consequences of this include the fact that obedience was demanded as a religious obligation—and was given by faithful Christians—even to those who used their positions of power in violent, destructive, and even murderous ways. For example, Martin Luther acknowledged that the German princes "do nothing but cheat and rob the people," but went on to call for the murder(!) of those who rebelled against the princes, since "nothing can be more poisonous, hurtful, or devilish than a rebel."[3] The obligation of the weak to be obedient, it seems, outweighs the obligation of the powerful to act with justice. In family life, women were especially encouraged to express their faith through their obedience. Indeed, the New Testament tells women explicitly to be subordinate to their husbands "as you are to the Lord. For the husband is the head of the wife just as Christ is the head of the church" (Eph. 5:22–23). The obedience that women, children, and slaves owe to their husbands, parents, and owners is detailed in the household codes of Ephesians and Colossians, and these passages were for centuries seen as central to a Christian understanding of the proper organization of society. Again, the obligation (for the powerless) to remain obedient was always seen as far more significant than the obligation (for the powerful) to act with justice.

For the most part, Christian preaching and teaching persistently reminded people of their obligation to be obedient and just as persistently refused to question the violent practices of those in authority over others. This understanding of obedience was not just lethal for Luther's rebellious peasants: even today, many battered Christian women understand the abuse they undergo as "divinely ordained" punishment for disobeying their husbands. Worse, many battering husbands understand their actions as sanctioned by the Bible.[4] The Christian emphasis on the redemptive power of obedience and submission "even unto death" has thus led not to redemption for women (especially not the redemption of their suffering or their bodies), but instead has contributed to their suffering in the form of beatings, rape, and sometimes even murder.

Thinking about obedience as the route to salvation leads to still more problems for women, other than the physical danger it can put them in. The perfectly obedient Jesus is contrasted to disobedient Eve, thus emphasizing that Eve's disobedience is seen by some elements of the Christian tradition as the source of all human sinfulness. Combined with the notion that all women are Eve's daughters, and thus share her impulse toward disobedience and her responsibility for the first sin, this is a tremendously destructive idea. To believe that women and women alone are the ultimate source of all sin and suffering in the world is a disaster for women, and for any hope of truly understanding how all of us, male and female, are implicated in the sin of the world. The repeated comparison between the obedient Christ and the disobedient Eve is a continual and depressing theme in misogynistic Christian literature. Eve's disobedience was used as proof of women's more sinful nature and justification for male authority over "weak" womanhood—and again, as justification for beatings and abuse. The third-century theologian Tertullian, as we saw before, was terrifyingly blunt in his indictment of all womankind: "Because of the death which you [women] brought upon us, even the Son of God had to die."[5] What an accusation! The destruction of humanity, the brutal death of Jesus: if these charges are believed, what hope can women have? Indeed, the idea that disobedience is fundamental to women's nature may also have contributed to the idea that redemption for women must be something different from redemption for men. In this scenario, after all, it is not hard to see that women need to be redeemed not only from sin but from their femaleness, which in its (disobedient) nature is fundamentally opposed to the redeeming (obedient) Christ.

Finally, the emphasis on obedience as the ultimate Christian virtue has warped our understanding of sin and the relationship between sin, suffering, and redemption. If obedience is the greatest of Christian virtues, then disobedience, or rebellion against authority, is obviously the greatest sin. And it is a sin that the powerless commit and the powerful (those in authority) punish, often violently. In the case of a woman who has been beaten by her husband, the sin in this situation was (and sometimes still is, sadly enough) understood not as the beating, but as the woman's disobedience, or failure to submit to her husband, that "must have" led to the violence. Again, we are telling the wrong story here: in this twisted version of reality, the violence that caused her suffering is not sin, but is instead a just punishment. Further, she needs to be redeemed not from her suffering, but from her own sin of disobedience. Telling this distorted story about the relationship between sin, suffering, and redemption is all too common, and is rooted in our insistence on seeing disobedience, or rebellion, not as Eve's *particular* sin in a specific case, but as a larger and more dangerous "original sin" that lives on as the root of all other sins. When (all) sin is equated with rebellion, we lose our ability to see and understand other kinds of sin—especially the larger, more impersonal and institutionalized systems of violence and exploitation that enrich one part of society at the expense of another, or that enable the powerful to take advantage of the vulnerable. When the sins of the powerful against the powerless are taken into consideration, our understanding of sin, suffering, and the relationship between them changes radically. Suddenly suffering can be seen as the result not merely of being rightly punished for sin, but the result of being sinned against, and it thus becomes something from which we might hope to be redeemed.

Another image of redemption developed throughout the New Testament is that of God's new creation, which comes to be in the work of Jesus. Recall the opening of John's Gospel: "In the beginning was the Word, and the Word was with God, and the Word was God. He was in the beginning with God. All things came into being through him" (John 1:1–3). Here Jesus, the Word, is the means by which creation came to be, and later, the means by which creation is renewed through the incarnation: "The true light, which enlightens everyone, was coming into the world" (John 1:9). Connecting redemption to creation does something very exciting: it widens the scope of redemption from the forgiveness of human sins to the renewal of the entire cosmos—all of God's creation. Through Jesus, all of creation will come to fulfillment. Creation will exist as it was originally meant to be, whole and unbroken. This wider view could help us reflect on larger issues of structural, social, and even physical causes of suffering: if redemption is about more than individual human behavior, then it is about wholeness, which certainly includes forgiveness but is not limited to it. Even more important for our discussion, the image of a new creation is not rooted in the *death* of Jesus but the *work* of Jesus (which may well include his death, but certainly could also include his life, ministry, and healings). For the woman with the hemorrhage, the idea of redemption as a new creation holds forth the promise that her body, broken as it currently is as part of today's creation, will be whole in the fulfilled re-creation offered to us by Jesus.

Finally, the last biblical image of redemption we need to consider is that of resurrection. "You were dead through the trespasses and sins in which you once lived . . . but God, who is rich in mercy . . . made us alive together with Christ—by grace you have been saved—and raised us up with him" (Eph. 2:1–2, 4–6). We have been saved because we have been raised up, just as Jesus was raised up. Moving the focus from the death of Jesus to his resurrection changes how we understand the story, and especially God's involvement in what happened. Suddenly God is no longer seen as someone who is pleased with a sacrifice, but is instead the one who would not let Jesus remain dead, and raised him to new life. Here we see again that it is perfectly possible to keep the same facts (Jesus died, Jesus rose), and attach different motivations, reasons, and explanations to them, thus ending up with an entirely different story. The image of God celebrated here is completely different than the one suggested by a focus on God somehow "requiring" the death of Jesus. The liberating, joyful, life-giving character of God is emphasized when the key moment of the story is not the crucifixion, but the resurrection. Certainly this image of redemption would resonate with the woman with the hemorrhage, just as it gives hope to all those who have struggled to the point of having nothing else to hope for but that God will raise them up.

Turning from this last and most hopeful of the New Testament images of redemption, we now encounter God the Liberator as seen by the early Church Fathers. Their understanding of redemption, which dominated Christian thought for the first thousand years of the church's existence, is known today as the "Christus Victor" theory of atonement. This theory builds on the ransom imagery in the Gospels and Paul, and on Paul's insistence that the death of Christ freed humanity from the powers of sin and death. It is, of course, not actually a "theory" in the sense of being a systematic and logical account that proposes to explain something; instead, it is a gripping tale of God's warfare with the devil for the liberation of humanity. While the details often varied slightly from one storyteller/ theologian to another, the story goes like this: All human beings were in bondage to the devil, held captive by sin and evil. A great cosmic battle ensued between God and the forces of evil—a battle that took place through the life, death, and resurrection of Jesus. Jesus was sinless, and so even though he looked like one of us (human), he was not the "property" of Satan the way the rest of us rightly were, and he was not subject to death, which is understood to be the punishment for sin. When Jesus died, Satan's power was broken: he had tried to take something (Someone) that didn't belong to him, and in penalty had to release everyone else. Some storytellers—perhaps playing on the fact that so many of the disciples were fishermen—even likened Jesus to bait and the cross to a fishhook: Satan, in his greed, took the bait and was thus defeated by God the Fisherman.

The thrust of the Christus Victor story strikes many people today as unbelievable, or at least as bizarrely funny (the cross as a *fishhook?*). However, there are some very interesting things going on beneath the weirdly mythological story of God finding a way to trick Satan out of keeping our souls. For example, the emphasis on humanity's bondage to the devil sounds rather fantastic to modern ears. But it is not so strange to describe ourselves as being limited in too many of our actions by our greed or our jealousy or any number of other sinful dispositions. Similarly, it is not strange to think of humanity as suffering under the weight of oppressive systems and social structures, and of being helpless in the face of evils too great to overcome. The only unusual twist added by the Church Fathers is that where we think of "systems" and "structures," they say "Satan" and "powers and principalities." They personified evil—they named it and located it—and made it more understandable. We do similar things, of course. Think of the War on Poverty, or the War on Drugs: neither drugs nor poverty is a nation with an army that plans to fight back; instead, we have personified a concept. It is not such a great leap to the mythological structure of "powers and principalities" that Paul mentions (Rom. 8:38–39) and the Christus Victor story brings to life. Despite the way it appears to us at first, then, this strange story embodies in many ways an interesting and appropriate way to describe much of the suffering that the people of the world endure today.

The Christus Victor story of redemption speaks to the reality of the evils that beset humanity, and celebrates a God who fought to free us from these evils. However, unlike our current understandings of redemption, it does not emphasize an individual's relationship with Christ or with God, or even focus exclusively on humanity and God. Instead, the Christus Victor story insists that God's actions in Christ were of cosmic significance, affecting God, humanity, and all of creation. This cosmic rather than individualistic focus is particularly helpful when thinking of the redemption of suffering, because so much human suffering does not seem to result from the specific sins of a specific individual but instead has to do with the complex failures of an unredeemed creation that includes everything from cancer to earthquakes in its everyday nature.

On the other hand, the problems offered by this story are also significant. The mythological language is perhaps not so much an issue as it might first appear, but one of the primary myths called upon in the theory—that of the Fall, and of Eve's guilt—has been mentioned before as problematic for women. Further, the story's focus on the devil forces us to consider one of Christianity's greatest shortcomings: its tendency to demonize enemies, to think of them as part of the armies of Satan and thus completely, hopelessly evil. Biblical scholar Elaine Pagels argues in *The Origin of Satan* that Christian rhetoric about Christ's victory over the devil was associated so strongly with Christ's victory over the Jews who, supposedly, rejected and killed him that the demonic and the Jewish became permanently linked in the Christian imagination. The centuries of pogroms, persecutions, and vicious hatred that followed—culminating in the Holocaust—stand as sobering testimony to the results of understanding the world solely in terms of God's people and God's enemies. Pagels goes on to show how Christianity developed the bad habit of demonizing its later enemies as well, and seeing almost all conflicts—religious or secular—as a continuation of the great struggle of God and his righteous army against Satan and the powers of evil. The danger here lies not only in assuming uncritically that we are "on God's side," but more pointedly, in our impulse to destroy utterly the people we understand to be "on Satan's side." It is, of course, possible to understand oneself as "on God's side," working for the kingdom that Jesus spoke of, without feeling a need to destroy one's opposition—Pagels points to the work of Martin Luther King Jr. as an example—but given the long Christian history of crusades, persecution of heretics, the burning of witches, and the Inquisition, the danger she speaks of is real. It is too easy to see Satan in our enemies, and thus to forget that our enemies, too, are children of God.[6]

Finally, feminist theologians object to how God's power is portrayed in the Christus Victor story. Here, God has the power to conquer sin and death no matter what people do, and God uses that power without any reference to human choice or freedom. Feminists argue that describing God's power as being that one-sided, even coercive, is simply wrong. What about human freedom? Moreover, if God's coercive power has destroyed sin and death forever, how do we explain the continuing power of sin and death in our lives? Christus Victor has no answer. Theologian Pamela Dickey Young, however, suggests that there is a way to understand God's power that leads to clear answers to both questions. She argues for a view of God's power as *relational* instead of coercive.[7] This means that some sort of *human response* is needed for redemption to happen; the action is not solely God's. Most theologians dismiss the idea that redemption requires human participation; they argue that this diminishes the power and freedom of God. But Young and other feminist theologians think that emphasizing God's power and freedom to the complete exclusion of human freedom means understanding God (wrongly) as a tyrant, imposing his will on us simply because he can. They point to the Gospels, where the power of God in Jesus invites, not commands, and where healing change is a possibility when God's grace is both offered and accepted:

> In the Gospel stories, we repeatedly hear of those whose lives were changed by the grace of God. . . . There is testimony to the power of this grace over and over again in the stories of the people who, in their encounters with Jesus, experienced sin, evil, and death powerfully overcome by God's grace. . . . But God's act seeks response. Unless I respond to God's gracious gift, I cannot see the grace that God offers as the power and the possibility to mend the brokenness. Unless I accept the offer of forgiveness, I still live as though I am unforgiven; I live brokenly; I live without integrity.[8]

Young's understanding of the human response involved in redemption helps us make sense of the story of the woman with the hemorrhage in a way that the Christus Victor story alone cannot. Her healing, after all, was not simply a matter between Jesus and Satan, with the woman as a bystander to the battle. God's power did not simply flash out from on high, healing her without her knowledge or consent; rather, *she reached out* and touched the hem of Jesus' garment. Her gesture was her response to the presence and power of God that she saw in Jesus; her choices were part of her healing.

In its understanding of the power of God and in many other ways, then, the Christus Victor story is clearly not the story that women today can turn to for hope and comfort. Its unfamiliar mythology, destructive use of the story of Eve, and the historically all-too-real impulse to carry the story's "cosmic war with the devil" theme to other situations combine to make the story unworkable for us, despite some promising elements in its vision of God as Liberator and of people as living in bondage to evil.

The next story of redemption to capture the imagination of Christians everywhere was told by Anselm of Canterbury, and is known as the "satisfaction theory." Here we find a much different set of possibilities for telling the story of our redemption—and more problems. Writing in the eleventh century, Anselm rooted his understanding of the atonement in medieval theology describing the three-part nature of the sacrament of penance.

When a wrong has been done, it is not enough simply to say that one is sorry (confession); rather, one must confess the wrong, feel contrition, and make satisfaction. It is this last aspect of penance that Anselm focused on in his theory of atonement, and its common name, the satisfaction theory, reflects this.

Anselm argued that paying ransom to the devil did not at all explain the significance of Jesus' death, and in fact obscured the true meaning of the death by focusing our interest in the wrong direction. It is not the devil who receives ransom, but God who receives satisfaction for the sins of humanity.[9] Notice that Anselm is changing the *story* significantly, while holding onto the agreed-upon *image* of Jesus' death serving as a payment, or ransom. The story Anselm told goes like this: Every sin is an offense against God and against the honor of God. As sinners, then, we have robbed God of his honor and must pay it back. However, we have no way to pay satisfaction to God for dishonoring him; everything we have, as creatures, is already owed to our Creator. One way out of this dilemma would be for God to mercifully forgive the unpayable debt, but Anselm argued that this would be wrong. "It is not right to cancel sin without compensation or punishment," Anselm insists. "If it be not punished, then it is passed by undischarged . . . it is not fitting for God to pass over any-thing in His kingdom undischarged."[10] Leaving something "undis-charged" means leaving God's kingdom less than perfectly ordered, and Anselm is deeply concerned with the perfection of God's moral order—and the threat of moral chaos.

This dilemma (not only the unpayable debt, but also the fact that the debt has forever parted people from the company of God) is solved by Jesus, the God-man, who lived a life of perfect obedience. Because he was perfectly obedient and free from sin, death—sin's punishment—had no claim on him, and thus his death was sufficient to make the satisfaction required for humanity's reconciliation with God. "But he freely offered to the Father what there was no need of his ever losing, and paid for sinners what he owed not for himself," Anselm explains.[11] In offering his life to God, Jesus discharged the debt that humans owed to God because of their sin. Justice was thus satisfied, and God's honor maintained.

Criticisms of Anselm's theory, and his story, abound. Even during Anselm's lifetime—and ever since—there have been theologians who attacked the idea that justice requires punishment. Besides this basic con-cern, theologians have also argued that his focus on God's honor and the need to protect and restore it makes God seem oddly self-involved, capri-cious, and even cruel. Further, Anselm's inability to imagine God's com-passion as working with instead of against God's justice leaves us with a portrait of God as a tyrant. Finally, as theologian Jane McAvoy points out, in Anselm's theory we find the work of God and humans strangely and painfully reversed: salvation is a not a human, but a divine need (God's justice and honor require satisfaction); and the work of salvation is not the work of God but instead a human action (accomplished by the fully-human God-man, Jesus).[12] This topsy-turvy understanding of salvation and atonement leads, among other things, to the notion that we are responsible for our own salvation, and that we achieve it by suffering and self-sacrifice.[13]

For our purposes, especially in seeking out the redemption of suffering, Anselm's theory is almost completely empty of hope or help. Anselm's focus is on the crimes of humanity, not its sufferings, and his emphasis on obedience and suffering as redemptive only serve to aggravate the problem he refused to consider in the first place. The woman with the hemorrhage finds nothing here, nor do her sisters today.

During the Reformation, Anselm's theory was modified slightly by the Reformers, especially Calvin, who argued not that Christ's death provided the surplus of merit that made satisfaction possible, but that in undergoing the crucifixion Christ took on the punishment deserved by humanity for its sins. This idea, that Christ was a substitute for humanity in its just punishment by God, is one that remains current today. Objections to this notion include the standard objections to Anselm—the problematic portrayal of God and God's relationship to humanity, the focus on justice over love—but go further, for the idea of making satisfaction is different from that of undergoing punishment. For example, paying back stolen money is different than going to prison for stealing it. The first, to a certain extent, has more dignity than the second; and the person who requires the first can be seen as fair, even merciful, while the person who requires the second can seem merciless. In other words, how we characterize Jesus' death has an impact on how we understand God: do we see God as bound by justice to refuse to forgive until amends have been made, or do we understand God as something like the parent who spanks the child even after the apologies have been made and the money returned, in order that the child "learn a lesson"? Frankly, neither image of God seems close to the loving, forgiving Father Jesus spoke of. Again, consider the parable of the Prodigal Son: the sinful son returns, confessing and contrite, and offers to make satisfaction, which the father refuses, and he certainly does not punish his son, but rather celebrates with him.

In contrast to stories that depend on ransom, sacrifice, satisfaction, or punishment, the twelfth-century theologian Peter Abelard developed a theory that centers on the love of God and on Jesus as a moral example to humanity. Abelard decisively rejected any ideas of satisfaction, insisting that:

How cruel and wicked it seems that anyone should demand the blood of an innocent person as the price for anything, or that it should in any way please him that an innocent man should be slain—still less that God should consider the death of his son so agreeable that by it he should be reconciled to the whole world![14]

Further, while Anselm could not imagine God simply forgiving the sins of humanity, Abelard thought it rather obvious that God's love was great enough to do such a thing: "Could not he, who showed such loving-kindness to man that he united him to his very self [by taking on human flesh], extend to him a lesser boon by forgiving his sins?"[15] After all, for Abelard redemption entailed not only the forgiveness of sins but also the granting of "the true liberty of sons of God, so that we do all things out of love rather than fear."[16] In other words, redemption transformed human lives by enabling people to live like Jesus—to live as sons and daughters of God, in freedom and compassion. Arguing that our separation from God (our need for redemption) was a result of our inability to love, Abelard understood that redemption had to be something that would push us out of our fear and self-centeredness into the new experience of love and self-giving. Thus Abelard saw Jesus as the one who called forth love from fearful humanity through his great love (including his willingness to die), enabling us to respond to the love of God.

Abelard's understanding of redemption as a loving response to Christ's love is an intriguing one from the perspective of the redemption of suffering. What is a loving response to suffering? And what happens when one responds to suffering in love? We recall that Jesus responded to many people suffering from physical ailments by healing them. Moreover, Jesus' healings were almost invariably accompanied by statements that the healed people then followed Jesus; in other words, having been healed in love, they responded by following Christ, continuing to transform their lives after their bodies had been transformed. The idea that redemption is not a single action (the death of Jesus) but is rather an ongoing process (as people learn to love) is also significant, as it more accurately describes the slow process of a lifetime of learning to follow Christ.

However, attractive as it may seem to us, this theory has been criticized because love alone does not seem to many people to have the "power" to free sinners from the consequences of their actions. Also, many people are very attached to the idea that punishment is necessary and just, and that freely offered forgiveness not only negates justice but is in some sense a sign of weakness (recall Anselm's idea that it is not fitting for God to pass over anything in his kingdom undischarged). Furthermore, others have objected to Abelard's focus on the actions of the sinner, rather than on Christ. This seems to give too much power to humans, and take away from God's power and freedom. Many theologians agree with the following, clearly disgusted, assessment of Abelard: "The Atonement is no longer regarded as in any true sense carried out by God. Rather, the Reconciliation is the result of some process that takes place in man, such as conversion and amendment."[17]

However, these objections miss the point. The first relies on our failure to believe in the strength of love, and our corresponding assumption that true power lies only in violence. The idea that "merely love" isn't enough to redeem humanity reveals that we do not take seriously our portrayal of God as love itself, and instead continue to believe that raw power/violence is truly at the heart of reality. Secondly, the horror expressed at the idea that humanity could be involved in its own redemption—rather than redemption being completely God's action—reveals a similar failure, this time the failure to believe what we say about human freedom. And, as we saw Pamela Dickey Young argue previously, to say that humanity must participate does not at all take away from the decisiveness and preeminence of God's role in redemption. Thus, to sneer at "some process that takes place in man" completely neglects Abelard's (and Young's) point that human love and conversion is merely a response to divine love, a response made possible only by that divine love. Remember that the woman cured of the hemorrhage took action on her own part in approaching Christ, and yet it was obviously the power of God that healed her.

The final atonement theory we need to consider before we set out on our journey never gained the prominence of any of the others, perhaps because it was put forth not by a theologian but a mystic—and a female mystic at that. Jane McAvoy, in *The Satisfied Life: Medieval Women Mystics on Atonement*, describes Julian of Norwich's understanding of atonement. Julian, a fourteenth-century Englishwoman, is known primarily for her account of the visions of Christ she received during a near-fatal illness, published as *Revelations of Divine Love*. In Julian's reflection on the atonement, she makes use of an image of the fallenness of humanity first used by Anselm: a servant who has fallen into a pit, and who is thus unable to do the bidding of his lord. This single image, however, is surrounded by two quite different stories: in Anselm's version, the servant deliberately flings himself into the pit in order to avoid the work he has been asked to do, while in Julian's, the servant is in the middle of performing his duties with eagerness (perhaps even over-eagerness) when he accidentally stumbles into the pit. In Anselm's understanding of the human predicament and need for atonement, then, humanity is clearly to blame, whereas "with Julian there is no cause for blame. She notes that she looked to see if the lord would impute blame to the servant and to her amazement 'truly none was seen.'"[18]

If in Julian's understanding, then, God does not blame humanity for our fallenness, what is the need for atonement? McAvoy explains:

> We still have a servant who has fallen in a dell and cannot get out. In fact Julian notes that she can see "no help for him." Amid his physical pains, she sees that his greatest problem is that he cannot see the compassionate reaction of his lord. So in his fallen condition, he can only dwell on his pain and distress until he is "blinded in his reason and perplexed in his mind, so much so that he had almost forgotten his own love." . . . Here sin is shown as physical suffering, and the effect of sin is the preoccupation with suffering. . . . Sin is certainly as real in Julian's theology as in Anselm's, but here sin is lamentable rather than contemptible. . . . To feel worthless, especially in the eyes of God, is the essence of sin. It is indeed dishonor, but of one's self, not of God.[19]

In order to remedy this wrong—to help the fallen servant see the compassion of his lord, and to know that he has not been condemned as a worthless servant by his lord—the "courtesy" of the lord is called upon. In Julian's revelation, the lord responded to the servant's predicament as follows:

> Then the courteous lord said this: See my beloved servant, what harm and injuries he has had and accepted in my service for my love, yes, and for his good will. Is it not reasonable that I should reward him for his fright and his fear, his hurt and his injuries and all his woe? And furthermore, is it not proper for me to give him a gift, better for him and more honourable than his own health could have been? Otherwise, it seems to me that I should be ungracious.[20]

The gift, then, of the life and death of Jesus enabled the servant to understand the courtesy of the lord and the fact that the lord did not blame him, nor think him worthless. Jesus enabled the servant to turn his face to God, to see the love of God. Jesus is the one who not only helped the servant out of the pit, but let him know that he would be rewarded for his efforts, not punished for his mistakes.

This tender story of God's graciousness to a hapless servant, fallen through no fault of his own but then blinded and made miserable by his assumptions about his worthlessness and deservingness of punishment, is certainly one that could speak to many people, especially women, whose sense of self and worth has been battered by the people and circumstances around them. The objections raised against Abelard—that sin is not taken seriously enough (i.e., not punished), and that love/courtesy is not powerful enough to transform our sin-corrupted world—would most likely be redoubled against Julian, especially since Abelard at least assumes that the sinner is at fault for being estranged from God. Is it merely sentimental naivete that would describe the human predicament in terms of accident and unjustified self-blame rather than culpable choice? I contend that it is not, especially when one considers the audience of the Gospels, and thus of Christianity: Jesus spoke to the sinners and the outcasts—people whose situation Julian describes admirably—and not to those already pleased with their status in the community and before God. The Christian message of salvation is directed toward those who perceive themselves as being in need of God's grace and mercy; such people, like the servant, often wish to serve God and find to their frustration that something in themselves or their lives prevents that. Julian, then, presents a very helpful account of the good news of Christianity, and offers much to bring with us on our journey.

It is now time to set out: we have taken our last hard look around our current home, and have packed up what is useful and left behind that which we no longer wish to carry. The wilderness beckons; new stories and new challenges await. We are listening for the voices of women as they speak of redemption, and we are looking for a new understanding of the role of suffering in our lives. We are accompanied, of course, by the anonymous woman with the hemorrhage, who found healing and new life by reaching out to Jesus. The powerful voice of Toni Morrison will be our first guide. In her heartbreaking novel *Beloved*, the mothers of the story speak of suffering in a way that makes it clear that the voices and perspectives of women have much to add to our understanding of this painful and difficult aspect of human existence.

Notes

1. Roberta C. Bondi, *Memories of God: Theological Reflections on a Life* (Nashville: Abingdon Press, 1995), 112–13, 114–15. © 1995 Abingdon Press. Used by permission. This book may be purchased at cokesbury.com.

2. C. S. Song, *Jesus, The Crucified People* (New York: Crossroad, 1990), 3.

3. See Martin Luther, *Against the Robbing and Murdering Hordes of Peasants* (*Luther's Works*, vol. 46), quoted in Darrell J. Fasching, *Narrative Theology after Auschwitz: From Alienation to Ethics* (Minneapolis: Fortress Press, 1992), 65.

4. Marjorie Proctor-Smith, "Reorganizing Victimization: The Intersection between Liturgy and Domestic Violence," in *Violence Against Women and Children: A Christian Theological Sourcebook*, ed. Carol J. Adams and Marie M. Fortune (New York: Continuum, 1995), 431.

5. Quoted in Mary Daly, *Beyond God the Father: Toward a Philosophy of Women's Liberation* (Boston: Beacon Press, 1973), 44.

6. See Elaine Pagels, *The Origin of Satan* (New York: Random House, 1995), especially chapter 4, "Luke and John Claim Israel's Legacy," 89–111.

7. Pamela Dickey Young, "Beyond Moral Influence to an Atoning Life," *Theology Today* 52:3 (October 1995): 344–55.

8. Ibid., 350–51.

9. Anselm of Canterbury, *Cur Deus Homo (Why God Became Man)*, in *A Scholastic Miscellany: Anselm to Ockham*, ed. and tr. Eugene R. Fairweather (Philadelphia: Westminster Press, 1956), 100–83.

10. Ibid., 120.

11. Ibid., 177.

12. Jane McAvoy, *The Satisfied Life: Medieval Women Mystics on Atonement* (Cleveland: The Pilgrim Press, 2000), 15.

13. Ibid., 16.

14. Peter Abelard, "Exposition of the Epistle to the Romans," in *A Scholastic Miscellany*, 283.

15. Ibid., 282.

16. Ibid., 284.

17. Gustav Aulen, *Christus Victor: An Historical Study of the Three Main Types of the Idea of the Atonement*, trans. A. G. Hebert (London: S.P.C.K., 1970), 146.

18. McAvoy, *The Satisfied Life*, 17.

19. Ibid.

20. Ibid., 16.

Chapter 2

TELLING THE STORY OF SUFFERING
The Mothers of *Beloved*

Telling the wrong story about Jesus is, of course, a symptom of a much wider problem: we tell the wrong story about a lot of things, including ourselves. When we tell the story of what it means to be human, too often we fall into the trap of thinking about what it means to be a man—more specifically, a man who is "free, white, and twenty-one" in a society that systematically devalues all of us who fail to meet one or more of those criteria. A young, pregnant black woman running from slavery bears little resemblance to the independent, healthy, non-disabled individual, accountable only to God, that we sometimes picture when we think about "the human" in the abstract. Theologians and philosophers have been telling stories about humanity based on this abstract, "universal" picture of a human being for thousands of years. It is that woman who has something important to tell us not only about what it means to be human, but what suffering means in our lives, and how to think about the complex relationship between suffering and redemption.

Some people react to suffering with fear, incomprehension, and panic. It overwhelms them, destroys their defenses, and leaves them unable to talk about what has happened. Others fight back: they react to suffering by naming their enemy and refusing to be beaten. Most of us see this second approach as the road we hope to take if and when disaster strikes: we admire people with "heart" or "guts" and look up to those who "never give up." We tend to see these as the only options: either you're a fighter, or you're someone who just gives up. In schoolyard terms, you can "be a man about it" or "be a baby." There are no other options.

But there is another way to react to suffering, one that neither folds up in despair nor assumes that suffering is an enemy that must be destroyed. Both of these approaches tend to see suffering as the star of the show, the center of the story. There is, however, a way to move suffering from center stage, while still acknowledging its tremendous power. This third approach is the one that mothers tend to take to the suffering around them, both their own and that of others. Intriguingly, it is an approach that grows specifically out of the *work* that mothers do (this will be important later, as we think about the work that Jesus does). Starting with the experience of labor and birth, a mother learns that pain and joy, suffering and new life, endings and beginnings are so tightly bound together that they cannot truly be separated. Suffering, then, is seen as part of a larger whole; it is something that *makes sense in terms of a larger story*. It is not an intruder in the natural order of things, one that must be eliminated, nor an inexplicable force that throws the entire world out of order, leaving one lost and alone. It is most certainly not the most important part of the story (or, having been through labor, perhaps no mother would choose to have a second child!). Instead, it is a profoundly difficult but quite expected and accepted part of the wholeness of things. With this in mind, a mother reacts to suffering neither by trying to destroy it nor by giving up, but by attending to its immediate demands (binding wounds, for example, or comforting the sorrowing, or breathing through labor pains) while working to shift it from the center of the story to its rightful place as merely a part of a larger whole. The work of shifting the place of suffering is work done through speech and storytelling, and so is of great interest to us as we ponder how to tell stories—not only Jesus' story but our own—properly. It is true, of course, that not all mothers react to suffering in the way I'm describing, and it is equally true that not everyone who does something like this is a mother. But this approach is easiest to see and understand in the context of the work of motherhood, and it is in that context that I would like to explore it more fully—specifically, in the context of motherhood as described in Toni Morrison's powerful novel *Beloved*.[1]

Beloved is the story of Sethe, a young woman who escaped from slavery with three children and bore a fourth on the way north, and then tried to kill all of her children, and herself, when the slave catchers found her. It is a difficult, painful, wrenching tale. It is a story in which it is very difficult to attempt the hard work of shifting suffering off of center stage, for as soon as one horror seems to be grasped and attended to, another surfaces, and another, relentlessly challenging the ability of anyone to cultivate a vision wide enough to incorporate such pain. Indeed, many of the mothers of *Beloved* fail. Even so, I believe that their attempts, grounded in their experiences of motherhood, suffering, and renewal, will help us think in new ways about suffering. This in turn will lead us to new reflections about redemption—that is, about God's response to suffering.

In order to look closely at this maternal approach to suffering, I want to explore it as it emerges in the voices of the mothers of *Beloved*, especially in Sethe's voice. She and the other mothers in this novel speak about their lives—their striving, their suffering, their healing—differently than do the men or the daughters, and that difference is what we are after. We will begin by looking at how the men of *Beloved* speak, and then the daughters. Both of these ways of speaking will be familiar to us: when the subject is suffering, they embody the "fighter" and "quitter" models of responding to suffering that we described earlier. After we examine these traditional voices, we will be better equipped to see and understand the new and different thing that happens when mothers speak.

Men's Voices

Naming is a powerful activity that shapes our ideas and even the world around us. Despite Shakespeare's claim to the contrary, a rose by any other name would probably *not* smell as sweet; or at least, no one would care about the smell if roses were called "rancidweed" or "slugthorns." The world-shaping power of naming leads many people to use it in understanding and combatting suffering: they identify the enemy that has caused the suffering, and by naming it, seek to control or limit it. After all, when an enemy has a name, he or she (or it) can be dealt with. When something terrible happens, we ask, "Who did this?" or "Who is responsible?" If we get an answer, our fear and dread lessen significantly. After all, "I don't know. Someone. Someone out there . . . it could have been anyone!" is much scarier than a simple, straightforward, "It was that one, there!" The process is similar even if the enemy is not human. For example, when the doctors don't know why you are sick, the insecurity of having nothing to focus on, nothing to name, is terribly disconcerting. Even if the name of your illness turns out to be cancer, that is often less frightening than a nameless, faceless, amorphous Something that cannot be fought because no one knows what it is. Naming your enemy, then, is one of the key strategies of someone who responds to suffering by fighting it, by seeing it as an enemy to be destroyed.

The activity of naming, however, is usually not limited to naming our enemies. The ability to name and define things gives shape to our lives, and many people rely on it to keep the chaos of the world around us in check. This was very true of the men of *Beloved*, for whom the practice of naming and defining things (and people) came easily. Stamp Paid and Paul D spoke often to name and define, even though both were former slaves. They would seem at first glance to have none of the naming and defining and world-shaping power of the white men in the story, Mr. Garner and schoolteacher. Yet just as Mr. Garner's declaration that "my niggers is men" completely transformed his slaves' experience of slavery (10), so, too, did Stamp Paid's decision to change his name transform his life and mission. Sethe changed her world through action (escape, murder) and remained silent for years about what she had done and why. In contrast, Paul D drove out a ghost with his voice, and named as his lowest moment the time he was forced to wear a bit in his mouth, and thus could not speak (71–73).

In looking at the tendency in our own lives and in *Beloved* for people to use their voices to name and define, we see a *creative* response to the world. Naming is, in some sense, using words to create what is named, in a way that calls to mind (although clearly in a much smaller fashion) God's creation of the world through speech: "Let there be light!" The creative power of speech is a sign of divinity and, in *Beloved*, of manhood: God spoke, and the world came into being. Mr. Garner spoke, and slaves became men. Schoolteacher spoke, and the men were suddenly not-men, counting for "less than a chicken sitting in the sun" (72). When Paul D spoke of Sethe as a young girl, she became one, acting girlishly in a way that shocked Sethe's daughter, Denver (12).

This creative response to the world is one we admire. It demonstrates power and control. It can, at times, call forth beauty in difficult situations. Responding to suffering, then, by naming and defining it makes sense. It is an attempt to have some sort of power over a situation in which we may be all too powerless, and it seems, after all, to work quite well. Paul D's body was assaulted by slavery and imprisonment, yet his voice had the power not only to name and shape his understanding of his life, but to frighten a ghost. Stamp Paid remade himself with a name. They fought back against the terrible circumstances of their lives and the enemies who had designed those circumstances and they won. Suffering did not defeat them.

And yet, it cost them dearly to name *as an enemy* the suffering that shaped their lives. It cost Stamp Paid his old name, his old life, and perhaps even his wife (we're never told what happened to her). It almost cost Paul D his relationship with Sethe. By naming and defining suffering, both their own and that of other people, the men of *Beloved* often *created* enemies (in order to destroy them) where there were none before. For

example, Paul D decided that the ghost child was an enemy who needed
to be driven out of Sethe's home, but that ghost, troublesome as it was,
was not an enemy. Instead, it was Sethe's only link to a child long dead.
Even more disturbing, naming *destroys* as often as it creates. It can be used
to define certain things as, quite simply, out of bounds. Some things are
not acceptable; they are named as such, or (better) left unnamed, unspoken, and thus nonexistent. These two issues—the destructive power of
naming, and the fact that naming can create enemies—call for further
investigation. Could it be true that using the power of naming and defining to fight back against suffering causes more problems than it solves? If
so, we would have to let go of this strategy we admire so much, and that
would be hard. To begin to explore the dynamic between the creative and
destructive powers of naming, then, we turn to Paul D, one of Sethe's dearest friends from her time as a slave at Sweet Home.

Paul D could not speak of suffering, so he shouted and sang. His "loud
male voice" (37) rid Sethe's home of the troublesome yet beloved ghost of
the baby she had killed years before. With Paul D's arrival, the house was
emptied of the sound of baby feet pattering on the stairs and filled instead
with songs that were "too loud" and had "too much power" (40). Paul
D's voice was also a voice of order, of rational control, and a voice that
proclaimed a profound misunderstanding of Sethe even as it affirmed his
love and care for her. Paul D used his voice to define his world, as far as
that was in his power (it often was not), and his voice defined Sethe as
something intensely other, something not even human. On hearing that
she had murdered her daughter rather than let her be returned to slavery,
he responds by attacking Sethe's understanding of mother love (hers is
"too thick" [164]) and by calling her behavior animal-like through his
reminder, "You got two feet, Sethe, not four" (165). In both Paul D's
actions and words, we see the destructive power of naming. Certain
behavior—Sethe's—was out of bounds, unacceptable, unredeemable. And
certain problems—the baby ghost—were simply enemies. He "solved" the
problem of Sethe's ghost by eliminating it, and just as the ghost resurfaced
as the girl Beloved, so, too, do problems named into nonexistence often
resurface in new, more frightening forms.

Yet naming things out of existence was not the worst of Paul D's mistakes. He also *mis-named* the people around him—never with malice, but
never with openness to other people's names, definitions, or understandings, either. For him, and for most of the other men in the novel, naming
was taken for granted, the obvious way to interact with the world. His
first words to Sethe were, "How you been, girl, besides barefoot?" (6).

Calling attention to the impropriety of her state of (un)dress, even in a joking manner, set him up as the arbiter of what was proper and improper: he used his voice to define Sethe outside of an arbitrary boundary that he chose. Later, his first words to Denver denied her age and maturity: "Last time I saw your mama, you were pushing out the front of her dress" (11). This statement—again, made in a joking, good-humored way, named Denver as a child in his mind—a baby, even, and established his authority as one who knew a part of her past that she could never know. Both Sethe and Denver were changed by Paul D's assessment of them. Sethe began to look and speak like a young girl again, and Denver reacted in rudeness to the threat she felt (8–14). Paul D's power to name and describe is clearly no small thing; indeed, it is a power that gets at the root of who people are and how they conduct themselves in the world. The problem is, of course, that if you name something *wrongly*, you will never be able to truly see or understand it.

And this problem plagued Paul D. While he could (attempt to) name the women in his life, he had no name for the suffering that they underwent, and thus could not understand it—or, ultimately, them. Paul D experienced suffering in the abuse rained on his body and the silence imposed on him by an iron bit: he understood suffering to be a *physical* happening. Sethe, on the other hand, found suffering not so much in the physical abuse she endured, but in the denial of her ability to act like a mother. This contrast is best illustrated in Paul D's discussion with Sethe about her experiences immediately prior to her escape from Sweet Home. Sethe's focus is on her identity as a mother and her rights as a mother, but Paul D is unable to hear this aspect of the story:

> "I had milk," she said. "I was pregnant with Denver but I had milk for my baby girl. . . . After I left you, those boys came in there and took my milk. That's what they came in there for. Held me down and took it. I told Mrs. Garner on em. She had that lump and couldn't speak but her eyes rolled out tears. Them boys found out I told on em. Schoolteacher made one open up my back, and when it closed it made a tree. It grows there still."
>
> "They used cowhide on you?"
>
> "And they took my milk."
>
> "They beat you and you was pregnant?"
>
> "And they took my milk!" (16–7).

This exchange, in which Sethe is completely focused on the horror of her milk being stolen and Paul D is equally focused on the horror of her being beaten, shows how little Paul D truly understood Sethe, for all his caring and the fact that "there was something blessed in his manner" (17). Paul D is presented as a compassionate, caring man who ultimately is the means of Sethe's recovery at the end of the novel, but he and Sethe understood not only the world but their very selves in startlingly different ways. He defined suffering as being beaten, being chained up, and wearing a bit in his mouth. These were his experiences; they were terrible, and they defined for him what the depths of hell were like. He knew what it was like to have his very self assaulted by the ravages of slavery, yet because that assault for Sethe came through her identity as a mother, he was unable to hear or understand her lament. Suffering meant bleeding and pain and bruises and humiliation; how could having one's milk taken away be more significant than being beaten? For Sethe, it was because it robbed her of her ability to feed her child: it robbed her of her identity as a mother. Paul D, who saw Sethe first as an attractive young girl and later as an attractive widow, did not understand the centrality of motherhood to Sethe's very being. In this encounter, he had not named her as a mother, and so her despair *as a mother* made no sense to him.

The creative power of naming, then, causes all sorts of problems when it runs solidly into the reality of people or things that already have names. And it often fails outright when confronted with *other people's* suffering, because the voice that names often does not want to listen. In *Beloved*, the men were much better at naming than at listening, and they were rarely able to listen long enough to see or understand someone else's view of the world. This is a criticism but not a condemnation of men like Stamp Paid and Paul D; they were under extraordinary pressure and did amazing things in awful times. Yet we would do well *not* to emulate their strategy of facing down the suffering in their lives. Perhaps we, too, will someday find ourselves in a situation so ghastly that confronting the world solely from the perspective of our own suffering is all we can do, but most of us will not find ourselves there. And so we cannot afford to deal with our own suffering by negating someone else's, nor can we afford to create enemies in a world already awash in destruction. Instead, we need to find a way to deal with our own suffering *in the midst of* the great and wide suffering that plagues so much of the rest of the world. We need to listen first, rather than leap forward with names, definitions, and solutions. The voices of the men of *Beloved* were powerful voices, but the voices of the mothers rang with a different power. Before we approach the voices of mothers, however, we still need to examine the voices of the daughters of the novel, especially the voice of Sethe, who is of course both mother and daughter.

Voices of Daughters

Earlier we discussed the schoolyard understanding of one's options when confronted with suffering: you can "be a man about it," or "be a baby." The men of *Beloved* chose to fight the suffering in their lives: they adopted the powerful strategy of naming their suffering in order to limit and control the power it had over them. They succeeded in defeating the suffering, but they also defeated a part of themselves. You might expect that the daughters chose a different route, and met suffering as their mothers did, but this is not the case. None of the daughters of *Beloved* spoke of suffering as part of a larger story. None of them tried to attend to the chaos while refusing to let it be the center of their lives. Instead, the daughters of *Beloved* either gave up completely, or they followed their fathers.

Beloved, the ghost-girl, was not a fighter. She collapsed in the face of suffering, and was unable to cope. Her voice—in its confusion and its strange silence—reveals a lost, complaining child, with none of the maturity one would expect of a twenty-year-old young woman. The strangest thing about Beloved is that, while she is central to almost everything that happens in the novel, she is nearly always silent. The reader retains the impression of silence even when she speaks, for her end of a conversation is usually summarized instead of quoted, even when we have the exact words of the other speakers. The few sentences she does speak are short and broken. It is no surprise, then, at the end of the novel, when the reader is told in the epilogue that those who knew her and lived with her "realized they couldn't remember or repeat a single thing she said, and began to believe that, other than what they themselves were thinking, she hadn't said anything at all"(274).

This silence is the mark of being defeated. The silent one makes no attempt to influence or shape the world: the world is too big and overwhelming. Suffering, especially, is far too large and overwhelming to cope with. In the end, Beloved runs away—an action that says, louder than her silence ever did, "I cannot take this."

Though her voice as a young woman is deliberately obscured from our consideration, Beloved makes herself heard in another way. She is clearly linked to voices—perhaps of ghosts—surrounding Sethe's home on Bluestone Road, known simply by its street number, 124. The novel opens with the startling, odd claim that "124 was spiteful. Full of a baby's venom" (3), and it soon becomes clear that the baby is a ghost, and the ghost haunts 124 by engaging in a relentless series of destructive, sometimes petty, and always surprising activities. It is here, through the voice of 124, that we discover the power of Beloved's voice, and the anger it holds.

The voices that surrounded Sethe's home "ringed 124 like a noose" (183) and were threatening enough to drive off Stamp Paid when he attempted to visit (172). He later decided that "the undecipherable language clamoring around the house was the mumbling of the black and angry dead" (198), certainly a category to which Beloved (as a ghost) might have belonged. This angry "conflagration of hasty voices—loud, urgent, all speaking at once"(172), while clearly audible, was as incomprehensible as Beloved's silence. The anger is clear, but the words are not: "the speech wasn't nonsensical, exactly, nor was it tongues. But something was wrong with the order of the words. . . . it stayed outside his mind's reach" (172). This angry but incomprehensible speech, while clearly associated with Beloved, in the end functions no better than her silence in responding to her troubles. We all know people who respond to their suffering like Beloved: her impotent, silent rage is familiar; her anger and helplessness ring all too true. She is the image of how all of us hope we will *not* behave when confronted with terrible suffering—the image of what we fear we might become.

Where Beloved is silent, Denver speaks in a straightforward, clear voice; and where Beloved fascinates in her strangeness and otherworldliness, Denver exists as the normal, non-threatening daughter with whom the reader can identify without trouble. Her words voice the reader's suspicions and ask the reader's questions. Denver, the daughter and reader of Sethe's story, is an ideal protagonist with whom to identify: a shy and lonely girl, she works up the courage to grow up and go out into the world in order to save her family. Denver has been called the most important character in the novel,[2] the one on whose shoulders falls the burden not only of memory but of hope. As the "site of hope" in this tale of terror and misery, Denver is in a unique and blessed position.[3] The reader can pity the broken body of Sethe's mother-in-law, Baby Suggs, feel horror at what Paul D endured, be fascinated with the mysterious memories of the ghost-child Beloved, struggle with a mixture of sympathy, condemnation, confusion, and rejection directed towards Sethe—and identify with Denver, whose struggles and triumphs correspond to the traditional psychological narrative our culture has constructed about growing up. And while it is not until the end of the novel that Denver is identified explicitly as "her father's daughter after all" (252), it becomes clear that—as daughters who succeed often do—she has always spoken in a father-identified voice.

Father-identified daughters, whose prototype is Athena (the Greek goddess of wisdom, who goes so far as to deny that mothers are even parents to the children they bear), have a strong literary heritage, stretching from Electra to Elizabeth Bennett and beyond. Denver joins this proud parade of women determined to break away from the weak and compromised female world of passivity and submission, not realizing that her mother—not her father—was the parent who could be counted on to fight back against the world's blows. Denver's father, Halle, after all, had watched schoolteacher's nephews steal Sethe's milk, and had not stopped them; instead, he went mad. Sethe was the one whose efforts to "out-hurt the hurter" (234) resulted in her remaining free with her surviving children.

Ultimately, Denver the father-identified daughter adopts a voice that corresponds to the male voice that names and delimits suffering in the novel. Like Paul D and Stamp Paid, Denver's voice rules certain things in and out of the conversation, and thus in and out of reality. This is most pronounced at the end of the novel, after Denver has been explicitly linked to the father she so idolizes. In a conversation with Paul D about Beloved and the possibility that she was truly the ghost of Denver's sister, Denver cuts off his words abruptly, not interested in his version of events:

> "Well, if you want my opinion—"
> "I don't," she said. "I have my own."
> "You grown," he said.
> "Yes, sir."
> "Well. Well, good luck with the job."
> "Thank you. And, Paul D, you don't have to stay 'way, but be careful how you talk to my ma'am, hear?" (267)

Not only does she refuse to entertain the possibility that someone else's understanding might aid her own (instead of challenging it), she goes on to take an assertive, almost paternal stance in her warning to Paul D about Sethe. Her words define Paul D as a threat, Sethe as a victim, and herself as a protector; most importantly, Denver's words define her as the one who will do the defining. She has found her way in the world, and it is the way of the men around her who survive by finding ways to be in control.

Sethe's voice as a daughter is perhaps the most intriguing of the three, since it is her voice (but as a mother) for which we are ultimately listening. It turns out that Sethe speaks sometimes as a daughter and sometimes as a mother, and that her voice as a daughter resembles Beloved's far more than Denver's. As a daughter, Sethe is a "quitter," someone who is over-whelmed by suffering and cannot find a way to cope.

We hear this most clearly when Sethe speaks of her own mother. Sethe clearly loved her mother, but remembers little about her, and her memories are tainted by a great legacy of fear and resentment. Sethe's experiences as a daughter revolved around the fact that her mother was almost never around:

> I didn't see her but a few times out in the fields and once when she was working indigo. By the time I woke up in the morning she was in line. If the moon was bright they worked by its light. Sunday she slept like a stick. She must of nursed me two or three weeks—that's the way the others did. Then she went back in rice and I sucked from another woman whose job it was. . . . She didn't even sleep in the same cabin most nights I remember. (60–61)

As a daughter, then, Sethe experienced the pain of abandonment, redoubled when her mother was hanged for an unspecified offense. This loss was intensified by the suspicion that her mother had been caught trying to escape:

> I wonder what they was doing when they was caught. Running, you think? No. Not that. Because she was my ma'am and nobody's ma'am would run off and leave her daughter, would she? Would she, now? (203)

In the end, Sethe's voice as a daughter resembles Beloved's. While more articulate, Sethe's voice, too, was the voice of a lost child: confused, resentful, and unable to extend sympathy (or even comprehend that sympathy might be necessary) toward her mother. Where the voices of men (and of father-identified daughters) tend toward powerful, creative speech, this childish daughterly speech is simply that—childish. It neither functions in a manner that creates nor redeems; one might be tempted to characterize it as destructive, but it is too ineffective even for that. Most patterns of speech are recognizable through the kind of world they envision or understand, and that of course is the problem for these daughters. They neither understand the world around them, nor do they have the tools to define a world (as their fathers did) in which they can survive. Beloved's voice degenerates into the mumbled incoherencies of a ghost; Sethe's into unanswerable questions.

Mothers' Voices and Maternal Practice

Where men attempt to create their worlds by naming and defining their suffering into something manageable, and daughters speak of their suffering either as struggling children—lost, angry, inarticulate, and afraid—or as father-identified definers, the mothers in *Beloved* produce a starkly divided discourse that can only be explained with reference to redemption. For mothers either speak to embrace all the contradictions of experience— suffering and joy, birth and death—or else they fall silent; they either speak toward redemption, or their silence points loudly to where redemption is needed. The redemption hinted at in the speech of mothers is a redemption rooted in wholeness, in the conviction that all things can be brought together for the good of those who love God. There is forgiveness implied in this embrace of all things, and healing, but the primary move is to gather all things together, and speak of them as all part of the same whole. The mothers of *Beloved*, when speaking this way, do not limit their suffering through careful definition and naming; nor do they strike out at others, laying blame or radiating anger. Rather, there is acceptance: not passive acceptance, but a powerful, determined action to realize and understand that the worst and the best of their experience fit together into a whole.

This acceptance is not an easy thing to achieve, nor is it permanent. The maternal voice of redemption and acceptance seems to come and go, leaving silence in its place when the hard work of acceptance has not yet been achieved. Baby Suggs speaks redemption in the Clearing; later, she sits in silence, pondering colors, unable to speak of a grace that would somehow have to include handsaws and bloody children. When she cannot include Sethe's actions in her vision of a world made whole by God, she has nothing to say. Similarly, the women of the community are wordless when Sethe is taken to prison; it is only when they find a way to include Sethe in the community that their words and voices are empowered to free her from Beloved. The maternal voice in *Beloved* is one that includes, embraces, and welcomes all things and all people, all sins, sinners, suffering, and sufferers; and when it falters, it is only in the face of that which does not seem (in human terms) able to be included, able to be redeemed. Silence here is the mark of brokenness so horrific that only God's voice could possibly find a way to include and embrace it; silence here cries out for redemption.

This maternal speech of inclusion and redemption is rooted in what Sara Ruddick would call "maternal thinking."[4] Maternal thinking, in Ruddick's terms, is the particular kind of thinking and reasoning that grows out of the work that mothers do—what she refers to as "maternal practice." The idea of a "practice" is an important one here: Ruddick points out that "distinctive ways of knowing and criteria of truth arise out of practices. . . . Practices are collective human activities distinguished by the aims that identify them and by the consequent demands made on practitioners committed to those aims."[5] Another way to talk about being a mother, then, is to discuss "maternal practice," for motherhood can be distinguished from other *forms of activity* (not states of being; the difference is important) by its aims and demands. The work of raising children, Ruddick argues, is a particular practice that gives rise to a specific way of thinking. Maternal practice "begins in a response to the reality of a biological child in a particular social world. To be a 'mother' is to take upon oneself the responsibility of child care, making its work a regular and substantial part of one's working life."[6]

Maternal practice, then, is concrete, not theoretical: it involves a particular child in a specific social setting. Moreover, a mother is not simply the woman who gave birth to a baby; rather, mothers are mothers "just because and to the degree that they are committed to meeting demands that define maternal work."[7] Given this, anyone—male or female, biological parent or not—can be a mother if that person chooses to do maternal work. But what exactly is maternal work? Ruddick identifies three key aspects of maternal work in terms of the "demands" that children place upon mothers. She defines the demands of maternal work as "those requirements that are imposed on anyone doing maternal work, in the way respect for an experiment is imposed on scientists and racing past the finish line is imposed on jockeys."[8] The requirements, or "demands" that are involved in being a mother are as follows:

> Children "demand" that their lives be preserved and their growth fostered. In addition, the primary social groups with which a mother is identified, whether by force, kinship, or choice, demand that she raise her children in a manner acceptable to them. These three demands—for preservation, growth, and social acceptability—constitute maternal work; to be a mother is to be committed to meeting these demands by works of preservative love, nurturance, and training.[9]

A mother preserves her children's lives, helps them grow, and teaches them how to be acceptable to their community. Ruddick claims that these demands are universal, even if any given mother's action in meeting them will of course vary according to culture and circumstance. Still, it is useful to reflect that the circumstances that shaped her understanding of maternal practice in no way correspond to Sethe's experience. As a slave, Sethe is trapped in a world where her commitment to care for her children often conflicted with what her owners wanted her to be doing with her time. Worse still, Sethe had to determine what it would mean to preserve her children's lives: did that involve simply keeping them physically alive, or did it mean keeping their souls safe from the ravages of slavery, even if that led to their deaths? Can it be a maternal act of preservative love to murder one's child? Ruddick never had to wrestle with the question; Sethe had only seconds to decide. This is not to say that Ruddick's theories do not apply, but that Ruddick was outlining a general case for maternal work in "normal" circumstances. Certainly slavery is an extreme and unusual case that would push the general case to extraordinary limits. Clearly, "preservative love" needs to be carefully thought through here; "social acceptability" also becomes more complex, because of the divided communities (white and black) of which the child is a part.

Now that we are focused on maternal work, I want to make a slight detour before returning to show how the speech of mothers in *Beloved* functions in a redemptive way. There is a fascinating (but mostly forgotten) ancient Christian tradition that not only links motherhood and redemption, but speaks specifically about the "maternity" of Jesus. In this tradition, Jesus is identified as a mother *because of the work he does*. In Ruddick's terms, the work of Jesus is seen as maternal practice, and so Jesus is named our Mother. Knowing a bit about this tradition that links Jesus, redemption, and motherhood together, all at the same time, may well help us see better how the work of the mothers of *Beloved* is redemptive work.

Redemption and the Maternity of Christ

Identifying Jesus as our mother changes the story of redemption considerably. Instead of the story of an obedient son repaying a clearly defined debt in a surprising but legally acceptable manner, we have the story of a patient mother who—knowing that mistakes, defiance, pain, and struggle are all to be expected—reacts to her children with an unfailing embrace. Surprisingly enough, this second story has a long history in our tradition. Far from being the work of contemporary feminists, the image of Jesus as a forgiving, nurturing mother was used by the early Church Fathers and continued for over a thousand years. Some of the most famous theologians who spoke of Jesus as a mother include Augustine, Origen, Irenaeus, John Chrysostom, Bernard of Clairvaux—and even Anselm himself, who more famously gave us the story of the obedient, debt-paying son.[10]

Historian Caroline Walker Bynum, in *Jesus as Mother: Studies in the Spirituality of the High Middle Ages*, discusses the medieval drive to describe Jesus in very human and accessible terms, focusing on images and situations that everyone would find familiar. This understanding of Jesus was strongly linked to an understanding of God, too, as accessible, loving, and close to human beings. In fact, it was thought that the best way to describe God's relationship to people was to talk about the relationship between a mother and child. As with all fashions, however, the pendulum later swung back the other way, and as God's distance from humanity became a familiar theme for theologians, the notion of God as mother did not have nearly the theological resonance as it did before. In more recent times, the focus on the concretely male "historical Jesus" lessened any remaining drive to see Jesus as the mother of Christians. In fact, any notion of the maternity of Jesus almost disappeared from Christian consciousness for several centuries.

Given that the maternity of Jesus is, in a sense, a lost tradition, we need to discuss what exactly is meant by this seemingly odd phrase. There were, in fact, three different aspects of motherhood that were important to those who spoke of Jesus as our mother. Mothers were seen in very specific, physical, concrete ways as being (1) creative, (2) loving, and (3) nurturing. Motherhood is physically *creative* in that a baby grows by taking nourishment from the "very matter" of a mother's body: in some sense, the mother creates the child. The second idea, that mothers are *loving*, should need no explanation. Finally, mothers are physically *nurturing* in that they feed their "own bodily fluid" to babies.[11] Here it is especially important to realize that in the Middle Ages, people believed that breast milk was made out of blood. No one realized that they were two entirely separate substances. This led people to make the following comparison: just as we receive the body and blood of Christ in the Eucharist, so, too, does a mother feed a child with her blood. In fact, the bleeding wound in Jesus' side was often compared to a mother's breast giving milk. As medieval mystic Julian of Norwich explains:

> The mother can give her child to suck of her milk, but our precious Mother Jesus can feed us with himself, and does, most courteously and most tenderly, with the blessed sacrament, which is the precious food of true life. . . . Our tender mother, Jesus, can lead us in friendly fashion into his blessed breast by means of his sweet open side.[12]

The theology of motherhood and Jesus tells us that Jesus feeds us from his body just as our mothers did; that through the incarnation of Jesus, we are "inextricably joined with divinity" just as a child is created from the matter of its mother; and finally, that the loving nature of Jesus reveals a God "who bleeds and suffers less as a sacrifice or restoration of cosmic order than as a stimulus to human love."[13] When we view atonement from a maternal perspective, then, we see God as a mother hastening to reassure her children of her love, rather than as an angry father demanding to be placated for slights against his honor. In this understanding of the redemptive work of Christ, Julian exults that Jesus is

> our natural mother, our gracious mother . . . [who] made himself entirely ready in our poor flesh in order to do the service and the office of motherhood himself in all things. A mother's service is nearest, readiest, and surest. It is nearest because it is most natural. It is readiest because it is most loving. And it is surest because it is most true. . . . To motherhood as properties belong natural love, wisdom, and knowledge—and this is God.[14]

"This is God," says Julian, speaking of motherhood. What a powerful statement! And an unusual one, for our times and culture. Yet the notion that the work of mothers and the work of God are closely linked, even identical, persists, and helps us make sense of our experience of God's mercy and our experience of the power of a mother's love. In looking at the mothers of *Beloved*, we will see how their love and mercy not only echo that of God, but attempt to further the work of God in the world.

Redemption and Maternal Speech

The voices of mothers function in *Beloved* to call forth redemption in wildly broken situations. In the following discussion of maternal speech (and silence), we will be looking first at Baby Suggs, who lost all of her children yet still spoke ringingly of grace and redemption. Next, we will consider the voices of the women who did not inhabit 124: Ella and others in the community, whose silence contributed to Sethe's crime and whose voices eventually saved her from its consequences. Finally, we will examine the mother at the center of the story, Sethe: her speech and silence, her suffering and sins, and the way she gives voice to her experiences.

Life as a slave for Baby Suggs was brutal enough to have "busted her legs, back, head, eyes, hands, kidneys, womb and tongue"(87), which left her with nothing but her heart. That—until Sethe's arrival—seemed unbreakable. Physically maimed by the violence of slavery, emotionally devastated by the sale of her children and loved ones, Baby Suggs was still able to believe in grace and wholeness. Once free, she became an "unchurched preacher"(87), offering her heart to all who would listen. The Word that Baby preached was one in which laughter, tears, and dancing all had their place; sorrow and joy were mixed together:

Then she shouted, "Let the children come!" and they ran from the trees toward her.

"Let your mothers hear you laugh," she told them, and the woods rang. The adults looked on and could not help smiling.

Then "Let the grown men come," she shouted. They stepped out one by one from among the ringing trees.

"Let your wives and your children see you dance," she told them, and groundlife shuddered under their feet.

Finally she called the women to her. "Cry," she told them. "For the living and the dead. Just cry." And without covering their eyes the women let loose.

It started that way: laughing children, dancing men, crying women and then it got mixed up. Women stopped crying and danced; men sat down and cried; children danced, women laughed, children cried until, exhausted and riven, all and each lay about the Clearing damp and gasping for breath. (87–88)

In this mix of laughter, tears, and dance, Baby Suggs not only spoke redemption to those who would hear, she enabled it to come to life among them. All was whole: the joy and sorrow, the living and the dead, the laughter and the weeping. As people around her laughed and cried, she told them to love, and spoke about what it meant to love. She told them to love what is not loved in the world around them—to love themselves, their flesh, which meets neither love nor respect in the world beyond the Clearing. Her words, strangely enough, speak of beatings and lynchings, but these are transformed into reasons to love:

Yonder they do not love your flesh. They despise it. They don't love your eyes; they'd just as soon pick em out. No more do they love the skin on your back. Yonder they flay it. And O my people they do not love your hands. Those they only use, tie, bind, chop off and leave empty. Love your hands! Love them. Raise them up and kiss them. Touch others with them, pat them together, stroke them on your face 'cause they don't love that either. *You* got to love it, *you*! (88)

In her preaching, Baby Suggs spoke as a mother. Her words are at the heart of the way mothers speak in the novel. It is clear that her words and actions are rooted in maternal practice: that is, in the experience of caring for children through preserving their lives, nurturing their growth, and teaching them how to survive in the brutal social world of which they are a part. The words she speaks are nurturing words, offering solace and teaching to the people around her, people for whom she cares as if they were her children. Moreover, the words and experience she offers them are nurturing and growth-producing. She is leading those who listen to begin to grow into authentic self-love, something for which their experience in slavery and even out of it has not provided. As a mother empowers and enables a child to grow into the self-awareness and self-acceptance of an adult and true subject, so Baby Suggs sought to empower and enable those who listened to her preach. Her maternal practice, begun as a slave mother raising eight children, continued and expanded in freedom, where she had become "the center of things . . . [she was forever] giving advice, passing messages, healing the sick, hiding fugitives, loving, cooking, cooking, loving, preaching, singing, dancing and loving everybody like it was her job" (137).

Baby's work was first and foremost maternal: even though she earned money as a laundress and a cobbler, the great bulk of her time and energy was absorbed by the work of caring for children (including grown children). When Sethe arrived after her harrowing escape from slavery, and wanted to greet her children despite the late hour and her bloody, battered state, Baby took their side over Sethe's, insisting both that the children needed their sleep and that "Sethe was too ugly-looking to wake them in the night" (92). Then, of course, Baby set about the work of mothering Sethe—still a teenager, after all, and one who needed a fair amount of physical care in order to survive at that point. Sethe herself remembered Baby as the one who had "bathed her in sections, wrapped her womb, combed her hair, oiled her nipples, stitched her clothes, cleaned her feet, [and] greased her back" over and over as she recovered from her escape and all she endured along the way (98).

Despite her love and her wisdom, Baby Suggs reached a point where her maternal practice could not sustain her, and so she fell silent. When Sethe killed the crawling-already baby and attempted to kill the others, Baby Suggs was unable to incorporate Sethe's actions into her understanding of the world. Certainly she tried, struggling with forgiveness as a first step out of the morass: "Beg your pardon," she whispered to Buglar and Howard, over and over again as she cleaned them up after their mother's assault. "I beg your pardon. Lord, I beg your pardon" (152, 153). Her words indicate not only a loss of focus—why should the boys pardon her, who had not hurt them—but the beginnings of an acknowledgment that forgiveness was the first thing in order if Sethe's actions were to somehow be incorporated into Baby's world of grace, love, and redemption.

But Baby was never able to get any farther than that whispered, repeated phrase. Indeed, Stamp Paid realized that the problem that drove

Baby to her bed and ultimately to her death was that "she could not approve or condemn Sethe's rough choice. One or the other might have saved her, but beaten up by the claims of both, she went to bed" (180). If she had found a way to approve, she would have been able to continue to speak of a grace that encompassed everything, even cutting the throat of a child in order to save her from life as a slave. On the other hand, if she could have retreated from the demands of maternal practice and speech altogether and defined Sethe's action as definitively out of bounds, she could have regained a voice different from the one she spoke in the Clearing, but a voice all the same. But Baby Suggs could not turn her back on years of maternal practice and thinking, and so could not speak except in a maternal voice. Accordingly, she was silenced, and went to bed to ponder color until she died.

The voices of mothers other than Sethe and Baby Suggs are few in this novel; after all, most of it takes place when Sethe and her family have been ostracized from the community. The other mothers do not accept her, do not interact with her or her family, and so we do not hear their voices. Yet the other mothers were intimately involved in the tragedy that led to their exclusion of Sethe (through their silence as they saw schoolteacher and the slave catchers coming down Bluestone Road), and equally involved in the banishment of Beloved at the end of the novel (through the collective sound of their voices as they drove the ghost away and called Sethe back to them). Their voices, in other words, though appearing only in two places in the novel, are a significant part of it.

As with Baby Suggs, the maternal voice here is either a redemptive force or it lapses completely into silence. There is no middle ground. The mothers of Sethe's community, lapsing into the childish resentment of daughters after the feast at 124, remained silent as slave catchers approached Baby Suggs's home in search of Sethe and her children. Some justified their silence by resorting to renaming and redefining what had happened: it was not generosity that enraged them, but pride. It was not the smallness of their hearts that troubled them, but the largeness of Sethe's crime. Suddenly the story was not about a community that responded to generosity with spite, but about a girl so proud she could kill her own children and not bow her head in shame.

This redefinition demonstrates a complete collapse of maternal speech and practice on the part of the community. There is no drive to preserve or nurture here, only to condemn. There is no sense of obligation toward another, no attempt to accept and encompass and learn from a surprising new experience (the party). The mothers refused to let their maternal experience shape their reaction to Sethe, and so fell not only into silence but into a paroxysm of blame and resentment usually limited to children. The attempts to rename and redefine the experience demonstrate an attempt to find a voice outside the maternal; the initial silence was the loss of the maternal voice, and it was followed by a renewal of (a naming, defining) voice in a different mode. Overall, this process reveals a community as desperately in need of redemption as Sethe. The crimes committed by the women of the community, revealed in the failure of their maternal voices, are no less important than that committed by Sethe, driven in desperation to make choices no one should have to face.

The deliberate failure of the maternal voice here becomes especially clear as Sethe is arrested. The women who should have offered their voices in comfort chose not to do so:

> Outside a throng, now, of black faces stopped murmuring. Holding the living child, Sethe walked past them in their silence and hers. She climbed into the cart, her profile knife-clean against a cheery blue sky. A profile that shocked them with its clarity. Was her head a bit too high? Her back a little too straight? Probably. Otherwise the singing would have begun at once, the moment she appeared in the doorway of the house on Bluestone Road. Some cape of sound would have quickly been wrapped around her, like arms to hold and steady her on the way. As it was, they waited till the cart turned about, headed west to town. And then no words. Humming. No words at all. (152)

This loss of speech on the part of the community lasted for eighteen years. It reached its nadir when Paul D came to town: when he left Sethe's and had nowhere to stay, no one offered him a place. The senseless (childish) silence of resentment and rage had become so entrenched that it struck out at any who even associated with Sethe. Yet this silence came to an end at last, and the voices of women were the instrument that saved Sethe from Beloved. The reason for the sudden end to the silence and resentment is not made clear in the text, and is perhaps not clear to the women involved: "Maybe they were sorry for [Denver]. Or for Sethe. Maybe they were sorry for the years of their own disdain. Maybe they were simply nice people who could hold meanness toward each other for just so long" (249). Whatever the reason, the women of the community came to Bluestone Road to rescue Sethe, and they did so with voices made rich with care and concern.

Of all these voices, Ella's stands out. She had condemned Sethe and neglected Paul D, but when confronted with the story of Beloved, Ella relented. "Sethe's crime was staggering and her pride outstripped even that; but she could not countenance the possibility of sin moving on in the house, unleashed and sassy" (256). When others suggested that Sethe was at last getting what she had coming to her, Ella snapped, "Nobody got that coming . . . what's fair ain't necessarily right" (256). After years of judging Sethe and her behavior as utterly foreign, Ella finally saw Sethe from a maternal perspective that enabled her to judge with empathy. And it was, in fact, an identification with Sethe *as a mother* that enabled Ella to finally feel for her: Ella, too, had a dead child in her past, born in the midst of endless years of rape by her owner when she was a young girl:

> She had delivered, but would not nurse, a hairy white thing, fathered by "the lowest yet." It lived five days never making a sound. The idea of that pup coming back to whip her too set her jaw working, and then Ella hollered. (258–59)

Ella's judgment that "what's fair ain't necessarily right" is one that mothers make routinely; in dealing with children whose actions are pre-rational, responding to them with what is right rather than what is fair is a difficult yet essential task. It was Ella who first regained a mother's voice when speaking about Sethe; accordingly, it was Ella who convinced the others that Sethe needed to be saved from Beloved (255–56).

The women's rescue of Sethe functions as a re-enactment of their initial abandonment of her. In a sense, they do it all over again, and do it right this time. As they approached 124, they saw not what was before them, but the party eighteen years ago that had preceded the Misery: they saw themselves laughing and feasting, "young and happy, playing in Baby Suggs' yard, not feeling the envy that surfaced the next day" (258). Without the envy, they are free to wrap Sethe in "a cape of sound . . . like arms to hold and steady her" (152). Singing for her as they should have years ago, the women find a way to free Sethe from Beloved—and to free themselves from the evil they had helped to create:

> The voices of women searched for the right combination, the key, the code, the sound that broke the back of words. Building voice upon voice until they found it, and when they did it was a wave of sound wide enough to sound deep water and knock the pods off chestnut trees. It broke over Sethe and she trembled like the baptized in its wash. (261)

The voices of women baptize Sethe in their care for her; their maternal concern washes over her as Baby Suggs's hands once did. Their cry is one of acceptance (of a woman they had long rejected), sorrow (for their crimes and hers), and triumph (of struggle over the evil embodied in Beloved). Again, all things come together in the maternal voice: all is made whole, and redemption has begun.

Sethe, a woman who barely knew her own mother and who knew no other women to turn to for help and advice when she became a mother, is someone who might be expected to have been confused, exasperated, and resentful of the demands motherhood placed on her. After all, she had no experience of motherhood, no memory of being mothered, and no women at Sweet Home with whom to share her experience of maternity. Sethe remembers bits and pieces about her own mother, but certainly has no memory of anything so warm and fuzzy as "being mothered." In more formal terms, she has no memory of her mother acting to preserve her life or health, to nurture her growth, or to train her. All those tasks belonged to Nan, the slavewoman who nursed and cared for all the babies on the plantation where Sethe spent her early years. Indeed, Sethe's clearest memory about her mother is that the woman was not able to nurse her, and Sethe had to wait and fight for enough milk from Nan (200).

Given her history, and her isolation at Sweet Home, Sethe had no chance to participate in her culture's understanding of the practice of motherhood, for she was—as far as her experience went—the only mother in the world. This strange, isolated existence meant that Sethe's understanding of her responsibilities and actions as a mother was never tested against the judgment of other mothers—until she arrived at 124, and slave catchers were coming up the road for her and her children. By that point, Sethe had developed her own understanding of motherhood and a mother's responsibilities, and this understanding was starkly different than what others expected. She loved far more than she was "allowed" to, and yet her love led her to behavior that other mothers, even those who felt far less passionately about their children, saw as a complete failure of maternal care. Paul D worried about Sethe's extreme love for her children even before he knew of her murder of Beloved:

> For a used-to-be-slave woman to love anything that much was dangerous, especially if it was her children she had settled on to love. The best thing, he knew, was to love just a little bit; everything, just a little bit, so when they broke its back, or shoved it in a croaker sack, well, maybe you'd have a little love left over for the next one. (45)

Similarly, Baby Suggs attempted to train herself not to become too attached to her babies, knowing that they would be sold before they reached adulthood (139). Finally, there is Ella, whose blunt comment, "Don't love nothing," sums up the safest way to live in conditions as brutal as those faced by slaves and ex-slaves (92).

Sethe's maternal voice spoke in extremes, never having been tempered by interaction with others. For example, she spoke of her connection with her children in terms that make the reader wonder if she even knew they were separate from her: "I wouldn't draw breath without my children," she declared (203); and, "I'll protect her while I'm live and I'll protect her when I ain't" (45). Sethe loved passionately, and no one had ever discussed with her, or even mentioned to her, the terrible maternal balancing act between loving and letting go. She had never talked through the complexity of what it meant to love a child who is both your "best thing" (Sethe's description of Beloved [272]) and her (or his) own "best thing"; and so she plunged headlong into an attachment so fierce and all-consuming that it led not only to one child's death but to the flight from home of two others.

Sethe's maternal voice also spoke in unusual extremes when she spoke about life and death. While the other mothers of her time and place certainly believed in life after death, Sethe saw much less clearly than they did the line of demarcation between the two. Because of this, her understanding of preservative love was wildly different: it included death as a preservative strategy. Sethe's defense of her actions in the woodshed make this frighteningly clear: "I took and put my babies where they'd be safe," she explained matter-of-factly to Paul D (164). In other words, she was only doing her job as a mother, acting to preserve and protect her children.

Sethe's extremism in maternal behavior and beliefs, which underlie her maternal voice, might seem to indicate that her maternal voice would have no connection to the redemptive maternal voice described earlier. In fact, Sethe's voice is just a logical—if frightening—extension of it. Where other mothers spoke in a maternal voice that used connection, acceptance, and forgiveness as redemptive strategies, Sethe's maternal voice pushed this to its ultimate end, collapsing all boundaries in a quest not for wholeness, but oneness. Paul D saw this as soon as Sethe explained to him why she killed Beloved: "This here new Sethe didn't know where the world stopped and she began"(164). Sethe's identity as the only mother in the world led her to this mistaken understanding of herself and others: the wholeness of birth and pain, joy and sorrow, death and beauty, became whole only through maternal speech—only through the one Mother—only in herself. What was real in the world was a part of her, just as her children were a part of her. Even Sweet Home, which might seem to have an objective existence outside of Sethe, existed for her only in her "rememory," where it and its inhabitants lived on endlessly (35).

Sethe's maternal voice never failed as did the others in the novel: she never found any situation that left her silent, unable to incorporate its difference into the demands of oneness. Even at the end of the novel, when she has retreated to her bed and seems to be trying to die as Baby Suggs did, her voice remains, making connections and identifying all things as a part of herself. "She was my best thing," she tells Paul D of Beloved (272). "I made the ink," she also says, reminding herself that schoolteacher's measurements and judgments, written in the ink she herself made for him, would somehow have been impossible to make without her (271).

While Sethe's voice never failed, it never truly succeeded, either. Her extreme version of a maternal voice could not act as the redemptive force that the other voices of mothers did; rather, Sethe's maternal voice contributed to confusion, isolation, and division. We see here, as we do with the silence of the other women, the limits of the human aspects of God's redemptive work in the world. While maternal speech in its varied forms may indeed act in redemptive ways, it is ultimately an inadequate force to rely upon for the redemption of the world. Still, it is important to remember, in thinking about women's experiences of redemption, that a primary experience of redemption for many women is the experience of maternal work and maternal speech. Knowing that the work women engage in as mothers and the kind of voice they construct as they describe and continue this work are part of how they understand the redemptive work of God is a significant step toward understanding what women seek (and find) as they struggle toward wholeness in their lives and souls.

Finally, there is one more point to be made about that wholeness, and how we reach for it. Where Paul D and Stamp Paid cordoned off certain areas of their lives as Things to Be Forgotten or Things to Be Overcome, Sethe did not abandon or deny her past. Even her most desperate moments are part of the whole. Through Sethe and the other mothers, we learn that it is possible for redemption to encompass *all* of our experience. Redemption is not about getting rid of the bad to make room for the good, but the realization that the good is big enough to surround and change not only the bad but even the absolute worst into something that is part of God's good, blessed, and *redeemed* creation. In other words, *we don't have to throw any part of ourselves away*. This is a startling and new way to understand the relationship between suffering and redemption! In this understanding, born in the work and speech of motherhood, redemption does not cancel out suffering, but embraces it in order to bring forth new life. Once we glimpse this startling new vision of redemption in *Beloved*— a book of fiction—we then need to ask the question: does this ring true *in fact* to our lived experience of God? Is it possible that God reacts to suffering not by destroying it, but by telling a new story that somehow encompasses our trials and tragedies in new and unexpected ways? When we remember that Jesus was raised with his wounds—that the marks of his suffering were not cancelled out, but were part of him even in his new life as The Resurrected One—we realize that this motherly understanding of redemption is a possibility we cannot afford to ignore.

Notes

1. Toni Morrison, *Beloved*. New York: Alfred A. Knopf, 1987. Excerpts from *Beloved* are reprinted by permission of International Creative Management, Inc. Copyright © 1987 by Toni Morrison.

2. Ashraf H. A. Rushdy, "Daughters Signifyin(g) History: The Example of Toni Morrison's *Beloved*," in *Toni Morrison's* Beloved: *A Casebook*, ed. William L. Andrews and Nellie Y. McKay (New York: Oxford University Press, 1999), 41.

3. Ibid. 41.

4. Sara Ruddick, *Maternal Thinking: Toward a Politics of Peace* (Boston: Beacon Press, 1989; reprint with a new preface, 1995).

5. Ibid., 13–14.

6. Ibid., 17.

7. Ibid.

8. Ibid.

9. Ibid.

10. Caroline Walker Bynum, *Jesus as Mother: Studies in the Spirituality of the High Middle Ages* (Berkeley: University of California Press, 1982), 115, 126, 129.

11. Ibid., 131.

12. Julian of Norwich, *Revelations of Divine Love*. Translated with an introduction by M. L. del Mastro (Garden City, NY: Image Books, 1977), 192.

13. Bynum, *Jesus as Mother*, 130, 133.

14. Julian, *Revelations of Divine Love*, 191–92.

Chapter 3

MAKING OLD STORIES NEW
The Mother God of Exodus

Perhaps the most common way to tell the wrong story is to leave something out, something important—something so important that including it changes everything. In her ground-breaking 1960 article "The Human Situation: A Feminine View," theologian Valerie Saiving argued that theology was telling the wrong story about sin, and that the reason for the mistake was that theologians traditionally focused only on the experiences of men. Neglecting the experience of women had led theologians to overlook a very real aspect of human sin: the tendency toward passivity, toward letting the self dissolve away into the needs of others and the pressing concerns of the moment. Until Saiving's article, most theologians had defined the essence of sin as pride—an excess of focus on the self, instead of the negation of self that Saiving described. Both, of course, are sins, and both terribly distort humanity and thus society as a whole. But by ignoring women, their concerns, their lives, and the sins that struck them down, theologians had radically misunderstood the complexity of the human situation.[1]

Unfortunately, the human situation—the brokenness from which we need to be redeemed—is not the only aspect of redemption that has been described theologically from the point of view of men's experience alone. The experience of God, too, has almost always been framed in terms of how men (either male theologians or the male patriarchs, prophets, and kings of the Bible) understood their encounter with the divine. Not surprisingly, the God of male experience is almost invariably male. Indeed, in Western culture, the God of women's experience is also almost invariably male. Centuries of speaking of Our Father and Our Lord has colored the way we see and understand God. For many people, "Our Mother" cannot possibly refer to God—the true God, the Father of Our Lord Jesus Christ—but must instead refer to something else, some pagan (mis)understanding of God. Yet there are more and more women today who *do* speak of God as female: their Father is also their Mother. This newly articulated experience of God has a direct impact on how we tell the story of redemption, for traditional accounts of redemption are built on the biblical understanding of God as Father, Lord, and King. We need to examine how women's encounter with a God who is none of these things might change our ideas about what redemption is, why we need it, and how it happens.

The best way to do this, of course, is to return to the biblical stories that gave birth to our understanding of redemption. After all, what we believe about redemption is based on several specific, biblical stories of God's saving activity in the world: the book of Exodus, for example, and the story of the Passion as recorded in the Gospels. What happens to these narratives when our understanding of a central actor in the story—God—changes in a significant way? *Something* happens; probably something quite significant. After all, stories have a dynamic and internal logic relating plot, character, and action; there is no way to change a major element of a story and expect the rest to remain unchanged. A single shift in either plot or character sets off a cascade of changes, and the entire tale is affected. While some of these changes could be guessed at or expected, the most effective way to explore how a story changes is to retell it and see where the new elements lead us. In the Jewish tradition, this is done through "midrash," the practice of telling "stories about stories in the Bible." We will discuss this ancient tradition more fully later on, but for now, it's important to know that in creating a midrash, new experiences are brought to old stories, with the expectation that the resulting story will reveal new depths to the biblical tales, and new dimensions to our understanding of God.

In order to examine the impact of women's experience of God as feminine on our foundational stories of redemption, then, we turn to E.M. Broner's 1978 novel *A Weave of Women*,[2] which is a midrash on the story of Exodus. Her reimagining of the great story of liberation that undergirds all Christian thought on redemption places women at the center of the story, and emphasizes their experience of God as Mother and *Shekhinah*. *Shekhinah* is a Hebrew word designating God's spirit or indwelling presence, and it is usually understood in feminine terms. As theologian Elizabeth Johnson explains, this is at least partly because its Hebrew root, *shakhan*, "to dwell," is grammatically feminine. However, *Shekhinah* does not refer simply to a feminine aspect of God, or God's "feminine" qualities. Instead, *Shekhinah* names God as "She-Who-Dwells-Within, divine presence in compassionate engagement with the conflictual world, source of vitality and consolation in the struggle."[3] This description sounds much like a Christian description of Emmanuel, God-with-us—*Jesus*. This link actually makes sense, for another name for *Shekhinah* is Wisdom (Sophia), and Jesus was sometimes known to the earliest of Christians as Wisdom's Child—and even as the embodiment of Wisdom herself.[4] Again, as with the idea of the maternity of Christ, earlier ages seemed to have a much easier time than we do in recognizing that Jesus' physical, human maleness does not at all limit how we can talk about him metaphorically. If he is the Way and the True Vine, why not True Wisdom or Our Mother?

With *Shekhinah*/Sophia rather than God the warrior at the center of the story, Broner's Exodus becomes a surprisingly new tale. Her portrayal of women's spirituality within the story of Exodus will help us understand how women's experience of God as feminine shapes women's experience of God's saving activity. That relationship—between a new understanding of God, and our understanding of redemption—is, in the end, the relationship between character, action, and plot: between who God is, what God does, and how the story turns out.

Broner's midrash forces the reader to struggle with the question of whether redemption is possible without God as a mighty warrior, and offers a new vision of what redemption can be when the God of the Exodus lays down his sword. For the women of *A Weave of Women*, freedom comes not as a result of God's *activity* but of God's *presence*: when women tell the story of God's saving power, what we hear is not that God has fought for them, but simply that God is with them. Redemption is no longer a matter of supernatural intervention in the world, nor of divine deeds of great power, but of divine presence in the midst of human struggle, and divine partnership in the work of redemption.

A New Exodus

Though set in Jerusalem in the 1970s, *A Weave of Women* is not a novel of contemporary Jewish life. A careful reading shows it to be not a modern story at all, but a retelling of the Exodus story. The fact that Broner has chosen to frame her tale of contemporary women and their twentieth-century experience of God within the boundaries of Exodus gives *A Weave of Women* an unusual status: it is both midrash and contemporary fiction, and thus manages to make startling changes to tradition (the past), while at the same time envisioning a new future, especially for women.

A Weave of Women reimagines the story of Exodus with women as the center of the story, and this seemingly simple change of focus leads to dramatic differences from the original. The skeleton of the tale remains intact—*A Weave of Women* opens with a birth and culminates in the departure of the community from the place of their oppression—but all the details the reader would expect in between have been dramatically altered. The book of Exodus presents itself as history, where *A Weave of Women* cultivates the attributes of myth; Exodus highlights the story of a heroic leader, Moses, while *Weave* dramatizes the stories of each of the members of its community; Exodus tends to name its male characters and leave the female ones nameless, where Broner does the opposite; and finally, while being saved from death at the Passover is the final event preceding the Israelite departure from Egypt, in *A Weave of Women*, it is the death of one of their own that finally spurs the community to leave their home in Jerusalem/Egypt. Broner's persistent reversals lead the reader to recognize that the presence and participation of women in the exodus is far more than a project of adding a few names or surface details: rather, it is a radical upheaval that shakes the very foundations of the story, including the event of the Passover and the very character of God. The enormous shift in the climax of the story forces the reader not only to focus on the consequences of including women as protagonists and speakers, but to begin to imagine, as Jewish theologian Judith Plaskow has suggested, "how the foundational stories within which we [women] live have been distorted by our absence."[5]

That distortion, while evident in many ways at many different points, must be traced from the very beginning of the story of Exodus. The beginning of any story is an introduction to the world in which that story will take place. The setting, tone, characters, and initial incidents of a story provide orientation for the reader with respect to this new, fictional world: the reader begins to learn what is important, what is possible, and, most importantly, where the plot is headed. A given beginning cannot lead anywhere, but must travel within the boundaries delimited by that particular beginning. This seeming restriction on the creative freedom of the storyteller is necessary for a story that "works," or seems believable, because a well-constructed plot must be a complete whole: that is, it must have a beginning, middle, and end, and each of these must be linked to the others. That might sound simple and obvious, but it imposes real restrictions on a storyteller. The beginning and middle of a story cannot be a continual downward spiral of awful events and tragedies if you're planning a sugary-sweet "all is well" ending; the ending would look slapped on, fake—unless there had been hints throughout the story that a happy ending was at least possible. Likewise, a gentle and happy story that ends suddenly and shockingly with the murder of all and sundry seems bizarre, and is likely to be dismissed by the reader or listener as nonsense.

The natural flow from the beginning to the middle to the end is important here: Aristotle, the ancient and ultimate authority on how to tell a good story,[6] insists that the best plots are those in which the action flows probably or inevitably from one point to the next. This does not have to mean that plots must be boring and predictable. On the contrary, Aristotle makes room in his understanding of plot for both "reversal" and "discovery," and goes on to argue that the best tragedies (and, presumably, the most interesting novels) are the ones in which "the incidents are unexpected and yet one is a consequence of the other. For in that way the incidents will cause more amazement."[7] An understanding of the beginning of a story, then, is necessary in order to be able to judge where it is possible for the story to move through its middle and ultimately to its end. Keeping in mind, then, our ultimate aim of seeing what happens to a story of redemption when our understanding of God changes, we need to look at the different worlds proposed by the beginning of Exodus, and the beginning of *A Weave of Women*.

A Weave of Women, as mentioned before, reverses many aspects of Exodus. The first of Broner's reversals is quite dramatic: a change in genre, or type of story. Exodus presents itself as a history: after a genealogical (historical) reminder of the households of Israelite men in Egypt, the biblical tale of the Exodus turns to the rise of a new king "who did not know Joseph"(Exod. 1:8), and that king's fear of and subsequent oppression of the Israelite people. Broner, in contrast, offers the reader no history and no background to her tale. It begins *in medias res*, that is, right in the middle of the action, as myths typically do. This sort of beginning jumps right in without bothering to help the reader get her toes wet: you come up gasping for air and trying to figure out who's who and what exactly is happening. Here is the opening of Broner's story:

> They embrace and face Jordan. They are turned golden in the evening light, like the stone. There are several of them. The weeping one will not turn to salt. In fact, she drinks her tears. She is a full-bellied sabra and her fruit is sucking away inside.
>
> The women breathe with Simha. Heavy labor has not started yet. They sit in the doorway of their stone house in the Old City. They move inside and breathe with Simha into the stones. (1)

Not only does the story open without background or introduction, but it is told in the present tense: "They embrace . . . she drinks . . . The women breathe." Broner's story thus acquires a timeless, mythic flavor, reinforced by the poetic character of her first paragraph, which uses highly specific, concrete images, colors, and places (gold, salt, the Jordan, the stone house, the Old City) to describe disturbingly non-specific, unnamed—even initially non-gendered—people (they, several of them, the weeping one). More importantly, the reference to Lot's wife—"the weeping one will not turn to salt"—both grounds Broner's story in biblical imagery, and signals her intention of widening what little we know of the stories of women in the Bible. And we know so little about the women! Genesis tells us only that "Lot's wife, behind him, looked back, and she became a pillar of salt" (Gen. 19:26). The biblical text not only denies Lot's wife a name of her own and a voice, but offers no explanation for her decision to look back, and no rationale for the deadly punishment she received. Many people assume that her fault was in not obeying God fully, yet Lot himself "lingered" (Gen. 19:16) when the angels told him to flee, and then argued about where he was to go, preferring a small city nearby to the hills to which he had been directed (Gen. 19:17–20). His lack of obedience is not punished but rewarded: the angels responded to his hesitation (his own moment of looking back?) by dragging him and his family to safety by force, and the place of refuge he chose was honored. In contrast, his wife "looked back"—perhaps in sorrow, in surprise, in amazement; the reader is never told—and for that single glance loses her life. We never find out why. Yet with a single word, "weeping," Broner offers us an insight into (one possibility for) the actions of this famous yet unnamed woman, and thereby recognizes her as a person instead of an enigma. She then goes on to repudiate the deadly message of the story, for the new weeping one, Simha, will *not* die, and will even welcome her tears as nourishment ("In fact, she drinks her tears").

Even more unsettling than the shift in genre is the change in setting. In Exodus, the Israelites were slaves in Egypt, but in *A Weave of Women*, the women live in Jerusalem. Jerusalem is, of course, the holy city, the heart of the Promised Land to which the Israelites were led after they left Egypt. It is thus shocking, almost blasphemous, to begin an exodus story here: how can Jerusalem be the place of oppression and slavery? For the women of *A Weave of Women*, however, Jerusalem is a place of fear and oppression, of injustice, physical violence, and even of the murder of infants. It is clearly Pharaoh's Egypt. Broner accomplishes two things by setting up Jerusalem as a new Egypt: first, she is reminding the reader that "the Exodus did not happen once and for all, that liberation is no guarantee of liberty—an idea that appears also in the earliest Jewish interpretations of the Exodus story, in Deuteronomy and the Prophets."[8] In other words, by setting up the Promised Land itself as a new site of oppression, a new Egypt, Broner reminds the reader in the most forceful way possible of a traditional yet easily overlooked lesson of the Exodus: the people (specifically, for Broner, the women) who were freed are in fact still enslaved.

This leads to the second point made by this radical change in setting: namely, that the traditional trajectory of the story, from Egypt through the wilderness to the Promised Land, is misleading at best. Its straightforward narrative line, "with a beginning, a middle, and an end . . . problem, struggle, resolution,"[9] does not in fact conform to what happened to the Israelites. Their arrival in the Promised Land was not really the resolution to the problem of oppression, for they found new oppressors there, even among themselves. The story, in a sense, did not end, but circled back on itself. Thus Broner's change of setting, which reminds us that the promise of the Promised Land was never achieved, leads logically to a dramatic change in the plot of the story: in *A Weave of Women*, the women never reach the Promised Land. In fact, the novel ends shortly after the women's exodus, as they are just beginning their time in the wilderness.

Another issue prominent from the beginnings of the two texts is Broner's reversal of who is named and who is nameless. The book of Exodus opens with a list of the Israelite male heads of household who settled in Egypt: as with almost all biblical genealogical lists, it is limited to fathers and sons. "These are the names of the sons of Israel who came to Egypt with Jacob, each with his household" (Exod. 1:1), we are told, and hear only the names of the sons, not of the wives nor daughters. The women are nameless, forgotten, of too little importance to mention. In contrast, Broner names all of the women of the households she describes. While the opening paragraph of *A Weave of Women* contains no names, each of the women receives a name within a few pages. In contrast, only one of the men is ever named. Even those men who become prominent characters remain known simply as "the kibbutznik" and "Tova's Arab lover." This deliberate reversal of who is named and who is left nameless is significant for two reasons: not only does it remind the reader of the nameless women of the Bible and their lost stories, it also emphasizes that this story, in contrast, is a story whose central characters are women and only women. Broner deliberately reduces the men to insignificance by denying them names. The "shock value" of this is enormous: most readers are used to women without names, or who are identified simply as "so-and-so's wife," but a recurring male character without a name is disturbing. It is only by shocking us into the recognition that leaving anyone without a name is wrong that Broner is able to demonstrate to the reader the enormous implications of the fact that most women of the Bible are nameless.

Despite this shift in genre, setting, and in who is named, the reader of Broner's story who has realized that this is an exodus of women might well expect that much of the well-known beginning of Exodus would be left intact. Consider the prominence of women in the first two chapters of Exodus: the main characters in the story of Moses' birth are his mother, his sister, and Pharaoh's daughter—all women—and Moses' birth is preceded by the story of two heroic midwives, Shiphrah and Puah. It is not unreasonable to expect that a modern retelling of the Exodus tale would hark back to this biblical affirmation of women's agency and women's importance: it was through the choices and actions of women—some of whom are even given names—that Moses survived infancy. But *A Weave of Women* reverses our expectations even here. The midwives in *Weave* are incompetent and soon replaced by other women; the mother is not noble, selfless, and silent, but an all-too-real laboring woman with "matted hair [and] parched lips"(3) whose voice not only cries out during the birth but leads the prayers afterwards; the sister is replaced by "wayward girls"; and Pharaoh's daughter is not needed, for the child (a girl, of course, not a boy) is not given away.

The changes Broner made here, where one might expect an easy fidelity to the source, point to the fact that reimagining the Exodus from the point of view of women is not just about "including" them. Rather, Broner takes seriously an idea expressed by Judith Plaskow: if women tell the story, there is a chance that we will not merely hear enough to fill in the gaps of the familiar story; we will instead hear an entirely new tale. In the case of the women who populate the opening of Exodus, Broner's changes force the reader to realize the heroic women of Exodus are not so much women as they are useful female actions. The stereotypical noble, selfless woman/ mother is embodied in each of the characters celebrated by Exodus and altered or eliminated entirely by Broner. The women of Exodus are soon forgotten, even within the story of Exodus: they have no individuality, only the stereotyped goodness of their particular female role to fill. The good mother gives up her son for the good of the people; the good daughter helps save her brother; the good midwives deliver healthy babies. None of these women is a person; none is allowed to display the complexity common to male biblical heroes. Broner's characters, in contrast, are complicated, interesting, and at times unlikable—just like Moses, Jacob, and other biblical characters whose stories we know in detail. The mother in *A Weave of Women*, Simha, is not a one-dimensional silent heroine but a big, sloppy, older, aggressive, single woman whose whole life was shaped in defiance of what was expected of her. No brave, good obedient sister cares for Simha's baby: instead, two frightened yet bold, angry yet gentle teenage runaways who have supported themselves through prostitution care for and worry over the child. And the courageous midwives are replaced not by the incompetent outsiders who seem to hold their place in the story, but by a startling group of "accomplished women"(3) from all walks of life, women who are named and described and whose stories are integral to the story of Simha and her daughter. They do not simply make an appearance and then disappear into the mists of history; rather, Terry, Gloria, Antoinette, Gerda, Hepzibah, and Mickey are continuing, integral parts of the entire exodus tale.

A Weave of Women, then, as an exodus of women, presents itself as a tale of exodus turned upside down. Its altered beginning already clearly points to a different ending than the original story. However, before we look further at the changes that reverberate throughout the entire exodus story, we need to take a closer look at the idea and practice of midrash, in order to understand the tradition within which Broner is writing. The practice of midrash incorporates certain assumptions and a particular history; both will affect the construction of plot and character in Broner's story. Hence, we will need to attend to midrash as a discipline in order to offer an appropriate interpretation of A Weave of Women and its relationship to the story of the Exodus.

Midrash and Women's Experience of God

A midrash is a "story about a story in the Bible,"[10] usually told to answer a question, clarify a point, fill in gaps in the original, or demonstrate how the original story applies to a new situation. The word midrash refers both to the story itself and to the practice of creating this kind of story. The tradition of midrash came into its own in the first and second centuries C.E., when the rabbis who were struggling to keep Judaism alive after the destruction of the Temple "did not hesitate to embellish, retell, reimagine, or even radically change the stories of the Torah."[11] Their reworking of biblical tales was rooted in the conviction that the stories were so rich, so multi-layered, and so complex as to contain all the information in the world: with this understanding, it was clear that by offering an interpretation of a tale, they were not changing the Bible, but merely revealing yet another section of what they called "the Oral Torah." The Oral Torah, given to Moses along with the Written Torah, held the same sacred status as the written text, but had been passed along only in spoken words until this critical time, when the rabbis wrote it all down in the Talmud. This might sound suspiciously convenient to us today, but the rabbis' conviction that they were not actively changing anything, but only revealing what was already there is an important one:

> Thus in retelling and rewriting these tales, the rabbis responsible for the midrashim were like jewelers who polished an immense and many-faceted jewel. Each generation turned its gaze to a new facet of the jewel, whose facets are infinite. Still, they were always certain that it was but a single jewel they saw, whose essential structure was eternal and unchanging.[12]

The work of the rabbis, grounded in sincere theological conviction about the existence and status of the Oral Torah, was also rooted in more practical considerations. The Temple had been destroyed and most Jews had been scattered from their homeland. How then to live as Jews, following the laws of the Bible? New interpretations of the laws of worship were needed, or else the Bible would have to be abandoned completely, as it seemed to have nothing to say about the new realities of Jewish life. The rabbis were convinced that the Torah remained and must continue to remain central to Jewish existence, and they worked to connect the ancient writings to the ongoing lives of their people. While interpretation of the Law was their primary concern, interpretation of story, too, was of great importance. The stories continued to speak to the people; the stories could be stretched wide enough to answer new questions and serve new purposes.

While the classic *midrashim* ("stories"; plural of "midrash") of the rabbis have long since been codified into tradition, the practice of midrash continues today. As in previous times, it addresses the pressing questions of how Torah applies to new times and circumstances. One of the most obvious areas today where Jewish tradition and practice is being questioned in new ways is with respect to the status of women. In recent years, the practice of writing midrash has been adopted by Jewish feminists who, like the rabbis of old, believe that the questions and concerns they have about their lives can be answered within the context of the stories that have always shaped their community. As Judith Plaskow explains:

> Assuming the infinite meaningfulness of biblical texts, the rabbis took passages that were sketchy or troubling and wrote them forward. They brought to the Bible their own questions and found answers that showed the eternal relevance of biblical truth. Why was Abraham chosen to be the father of a people? What was the status of the law before the Torah was given? Who was Adam's first wife? Why was Dinah raped? These were not questions for historical investigation but imaginative exegesis and literary amplification.

The open-ended process of writing midrash, simultaneously serious
and playful, imaginative, metaphoric, has lent itself to feminist use. While
feminist midrash—like all midrash—is a reflection of contemporary
beliefs and experiences, its root conviction is utterly traditional. It stands
on the rabbinic insistence that the Bible can be made to speak to the present day. If the Torah is our text, it can and must answer our questions and
share our values; if we wrestle with it, it will yield meaning.[13]

This conviction, that the Bible can and does "answer our questions and
share our values," has been shaken in recent years as feminists have wres-
tled with the words and stories of the Bible. Both Christian and Jewish
feminists have come to see the Bible and biblical language to be problematic
for women. The Bible, the liberating story of God's saving relationship
with humanity, is also a book that, as biblical scholar Sandra Schneiders
puts it, was "written largely if not exclusively by men, about men, and for
men."[14] It is often sexist, even misogynist, in its portrayal of women (when
they appear at all). Even more troubling, most metaphors for God are not
just male but patriarchal (king, warrior, slave owner); that is, they assume
and encourage relationships of hierarchy, domination, and violence.[15] The
problem, of course, lies not merely in the Bible but in how our religious
traditions choose to use it. There are, after all, some female metaphors for
God in the Bible, although they are few and far between. The question
then becomes, "Are the male biblical metaphors for God central to our
understanding of the divine, or are they one of several valid ways to talk
about God?" In many denominations today, the answer is that they are
central, even essential. Schneiders points out that in the Catholic Church,
"although male church authorities maintain that God is Spirit and therefore the category of sex does not apply to God, they continue to insist that
only male language is suitable for talking about or to God, at least in public worship."[16] This paradox—God is neither male or female, but to speak
of God in female terms is absolutely and always wrong—reveals the
misogyny at the heart of our language about God far more than the simple use of the terms "Father" or "Lord."

Some women, when confronted with the twin biblical realities of the
misogynist portrayal of women and relentlessly masculine understanding
of divinity, have decided that the Bible can only be oppressive and hurtful
to women, and they have rejected it, along with both Judaism and
Christianity. Others are trying to find a way to claim the "good" portions
of their tradition and reject the rest. More and more, however, Jewish and
Christian feminists are realizing that eliminating the patriarchal parts of

their religion and religious texts is not possible. Jewish feminist Judith Plaskow describes her complex relationship to her beloved yet often hurtful tradition:

> For better and for worse, Jewish history is my history, the texts that record that history are my texts. Abraham and Sarah are my ancestors, as are Elijah and the women who worshipped the Queen of Heaven (Jer. 44:15–19). I went forth from Egypt and danced with Miriam at the shores of the sea. Even where I dissent from biblical or rabbinic teaching, where I find it problematic, unjust, or simply wrong, I still see it as part of a past that has shaped and formed me. As mine, it is a past for me to struggle with, not a past on which I am willing to turn my back.[17]

Refusing to turn one's back on tradition both recognizes that the tradition, despite its failings, continues to have meaning, and that it is impossible to move forward without some grounding in history. While it is true that learning about the past can be painful for many women, it is also true that it is impossible, within a biblically based religion, to create a present that ignores the Bible.[18] As Catholic feminist Rosemary Ruether explains, we mine broken traditions for what we can salvage because, despite our yearning for change and reform, we recognize a deep human need to understand ourselves as living in continuity with those who have gone before us.[19]

The ancient practice of midrash offers women today a way to rethink the religious traditions in which they live, to find glimmers of truth submerged in existing tradition. To write midrash is to insist both on the richness of the past and on its flexibility; it is also to claim the truth of the present as valid and valuable, not to be dismissed as mere fad or fashion. Midrash, then, requires a balancing act between past and present, tradition and truth, that affects the storyteller's choices about both plot and character, especially if that character is God. In *A Weave of Women*, the story of exodus serves as framework and grounding for a contemporary story of women's experience of the saving power of God: by constructing the novel as a midrash, Broner is challenging not only our vision of what Judaism could be, but of who Yahweh was, is, and continues to be. "I AM WHO I AM," we hear in Exodus; some translate this statement as "I will be who I will be" (Exod. 3:14). By writing a midrash on this story, Broner holds the God of exodus in tension with the experience of women today, and asks, "Who will God be now?"

The Changing Trajectory of a Familiar Story

We learn who God is and will be through God's actions; that is, through the plot of the story. In Exodus, God is the central character, and God's actions not only shape certain aspects of the story but flatly determine the entire shape of the plot. In fact, it is possible to summarize the plot completely in terms of the activity of God: God hears the cry of the suffering Hebrew slaves; God battles with Pharaoh over the fate of those slaves; God leads the people to freedom. The beginning of Exodus establishes both the horror of the slavery endured by the Israelites and God's determination to do something in response to their suffering. By framing the beginning of *A Weave of Women* within familiar story elements from Exodus, Broner sets up in the reader the expectation that the story will continue in its familiar form: that is, God will respond to the suffering of the women. However, the middle of *Weave* signals a radical turn away from the plot structure that we expect: while the middle of Exodus gives us God's battle with Pharaoh through the plagues, the middle of *Weave* is characterized by a series of violent, destructive events—clearly plagues—directed not at an enemy but at the women themselves. Even more startling, at the center of the novel, the baby born at the beginning—Hava, the child who held Moses' place in the story—is murdered. Throughout the middle of *Weave*, it is not the power of God that shines forth but the power of darkness, or (in the terms of the story), the power of Pharaoh. The middle of the story strikes the reader as a complete derailment of the plot as it was expected to unfold: hence we need to look at the middle of *A Weave of Women* both in terms of how this middle follows from its beginning, and in terms of how the story as a whole relates to the original on which it was based. In other words, we need to examine the middle of the story to see how *Weave* succeeds (or fails) as a story in its own right, and we also need to look at what is happening at this point in terms of a midrashic exploration of Exodus.

Both Exodus and *A Weave of Women* open in situations of danger and suffering, but in Exodus, it is clear from the beginning that God was watching over what was happening. It was God who brought the Israelites to Egypt; God who rewarded the midwives for their courageous defiance of Pharaoh's deadly orders; and God who heard the cries of the slaves, and "took notice" (Exod. 2:25). Keeping in mind that a plot must flow inevitably or probably from one point to another, it is easily arguable that God's presence in the very beginning of the story makes God's appearance to Moses a logically acceptable event. It was certainly not inevitable, but it was also not beyond the realm of possibility or even probability: the beginning of Exodus makes God's interest in the events in Egypt clear. The beginning of *A Weave of Women*, however, does not portray any of God's activity, and this paves the way for a logically different middle of the story. In fact, instead of the activity of God, the opening of *Weave* features the activity of demons. The death and destruction that characterize the heart of Broner's novel, then, flow logically from the pervasive presence and activity of the demons in the beginning: the world of the novel is decisively shaped by the presence and activity, not of God, but of evil in the events of the women's lives.

   Demons abound in the world of *A Weave of Women*: a young abusive traveller is labelled a demon (48–50); demons are said to cause "exhaustion in the knees"(51) and other physical ailments; a few of the women even name themselves as demons. Demons seem to occupy a place halfway between the human and the spirit world, and are often unrecognizable except through their actions, which are always harmful.

   Demons surround the women, not only in the people they meet but in the daily trials of life. Dahlia, the singer, sees them in the running nose and clogged throat that prevents her from performing well (51), while Mickey blames demons for knots in her hair and pain in her knees. These everyday, minor irritants are given supernatural status, elevating them far beyond what it seems they should deserve. However, the women do not limit their understanding of the demonic to minor troubles. They also identify it specifically with human beings who do or say hurtful things: first, with the young man who responded to their kindness with pornographic verbal abuse, and then with themselves, in stories of their failures to act with integrity. The demonic, it seems, is both great and small, but in all its forms is injurious to the best possibilities inherent in the human. Thus Gerda sees the demonic in herself when she not only rejects love but is unjust to a student (54), and Antoinette recognizes demons in the classroom where her own weakness and fear led her to betray her scholarly principles (55).

   What is going on here? Why demons? Most people today do not think about demons, and certainly do not blame them for "bad hair days." What we need to realize is that the presence of demons is a rhetorical device that locates this story in the realm of midrash. What is at issue here is *not* the existence of supernatural beings in Jerusalem in the 1970s, but *the existence of these contemporary women in the world of the Exodus*. As modern inhabitants of a mostly secular world, we find it strange to speak of evil spirits lurking in dark places, waiting to tangle our hair, make us sneeze, or appear in the guise of a stranger merely to be rude. Such superstitions have no place in our lives. However, a world populated by unseen angels, demons, and even the very presence of God is in fact familiar to us: it is the world of Exodus, and indeed of the entire Bible. The world described and assumed in Exodus is a world in which encounters between human beings and supernatural, spiritual beings is possible, if unusual and even surprising (certainly Moses was startled, at the least, to discover God in a burning bush). Similarly, the world constructed by Broner in *A Weave of Women* is one in which communication between spirits and human beings is possible. Broner's insistence here that her characters live in a world unfamiliar to us reminds us again that this novel is not adhering to realistic conventions; this is, instead, a mythic (midrashic) place. Unlike our complex but "natural" world, the world of *Weave* is one in which evil and weakness have a cause, and that cause is the presence of demons. As Pharaoh is identified as the root cause of the suffering of the Hebrews, so demons are identified as the root cause of the sufferings of the women.

The suffering caused by demons escalates from tangled hair to beatings and even murder as the story continues, just as the oppressive rule of Pharaoh over the Israelites increased in severity over the beginning and middle of the Exodus story. Mickey's unhappiness, caused primarily by her husband's refusal to divorce her, is given dramatic life when it is portrayed as possession by a demon known as a dybbuk, or lost soul. The grief Simha suffers after the death of her baby is manifested in "a gathering, a droning . . . faintly wailing . . . hissing" that permeates her home, whispering of the death and decomposition of babies (138). Deedee is stoned almost to death; Joan raped; Vered beaten: the assaults on the women are relentless. The episodic nature of the middle of the story—first one woman, then another, suffers physically and mentally—reflects the episodic nature of the middle of Exodus, where one plague after another inflicts suffering on the people of Egypt. This is, however, a strange twist on the original story: the plagues, after all, did not happen to the Israelites but to the Egyptians. By the middle of *Weave*, the reader can only conclude that Pharaoh appears to be winning, and God seems to have conceded the fight.

The plot of *A Weave of Women* is thus proceeding in a way that makes sense as a logically constructed plot, but not as a true midrash on Exodus. Because the opening of *Weave* never set the stage for God's intervention in history, the middle cannot suddenly make what would be a startling and improbable turn, and so it seems that, in following the dictates of a well-constructed plot, we have reached a midrashic impasse. God has abandoned the women in Pharaoh's Egypt, and if there is a way out, it will not come through God nor through the special, chosen baby born at the opening of the tale, for in *A Weave of Women*, that baby is killed. Hava's death is both a murder and a mistake: the hammer-wielding fanatic who strikes her dead was aiming at Simha, and actually wanted to kill not Simha but Dahlia, who earned his fatal rage by being a Jew in love with a Bedouin prince. The confusion in the room where the fatal blow was struck echoes our own confusion at this point: if Hava holds Moses's place in the story, where do we go from here?

The death of Hava is nothing short of disastrous for the status of *A Weave of Women* as a midrash on Exodus. Her loss leaves the reader, halfway through the novel, scrambling to make sense of a story careening crazily off its expected track. There was no miracle for Simha, no basket in the reeds for Hava. How then can the people be saved? The novel's answer is as startling as it is clear: the women must take upon themselves the duties of both creator and redeemer, and remake the world on their own: "We must make a firmament between heaven and earth," announces Terry, "between reality and unreality" (139). This bold assessment of what is required of them implies both that Hava's death was world-destroying and that the heavens are empty. In midrashic terms, the story here—like Simha's life—seems broken beyond our ability to make sense of it. Yahweh is the creator; are the women to usurp divine power? This exodus story is no longer functional: it has shattered in agony under the weight of Hava's murder.

And yet, despite the fact that the familiar story of Exodus seems to lie in tatters at this point, the plot of *A Weave of Women* ends in a triumphant exodus. The women leave Jerusalem, and celebrate their life together in a new land. Under the terms of the original story and with any consideration for the logical flow of a plot, this is flatly impossible: such an ending cannot follow from this middle. However, the seeming collapse of the *plot* is an illusion born of our neglect of *character*: up until now, we have ignored the fact that in *Weave*, the central actor of Exodus, God, has been completely rethought and reworked. We now turn to an analysis of God in *Weave* and Exodus in order to see how a new understanding of God leads to a new understanding of God's saving activity. Once we see and understand God's presence in Broner's story, we will see that it is in fact entirely possible for the exodus to go forward even under the circumstances we have reached here.

Women's Voices and Biblical Language

We need to look at the character of God in both stories, but before we can do so, a critical problem must be addressed. Unlike the book of Exodus, in which God appears as a primary character whose actions and words can be analyzed, *A Weave of Women* offers us a God who can be known only indirectly. God never appears in direct speech or action in the novel; we can glean our understanding of God and God's activity only through what the women say and do about God. Their prayer, of course, is less an indication of who God is than of what their experience of God is, but it is also true that we are more interested here in their experience of God. However, because an exploration of the experience of God in *Weave* will thus entail an exploration of the women's words about God in prayer and ritual, our analysis immediately confronts a problem: how can we hear women's voices within a religious world that assumes the silence—indeed the absence and exclusion—of women, their bodies, and their experiences? Because of the traditional separation of women from the Word of God in study and worship, and because of traditional religious assumptions about the character of women, we have only a limited vocabulary in which we can talk "reasonably" about God. In fact, we have constructed an understanding of God (as transcendent, disembodied Other) that makes it almost impossible to hear women talk about their experience of God *as feminine*—as immanent, intimate, embodied—without presuming that they are in fact talking about something else entirely: ancient pagan goddesses, perhaps, or Mother Nature. We need to set aside this reaction if we are to explore adequately Simha's understanding of God in *Weave*; we need to recognize that her prayer, however unorthodox in form and language, is in fact part of the unfolding Jewish tradition of prayer and conversation with God. In order to do that, we need to grasp a paradox: women's experience is not part of the biblical tradition, but the biblical tradition is part of women's experience. As explained by Jewish feminist Tikva Frymer-Kensky, this means that Jewish women today are (and should be) in the midst of wrestling with and transforming their texts and traditions:

> My own religious understanding and spiritual quest have been shaped by thousands of years of Jewish tradition, as well as by my own personal experiences and the events and learning of the modern world. I do not want to leave my own religious tradition in order to express my femaleness. I do not want to spend Sabbath at synagogue and give birth in a coven. To do so would re-create and perpetuate the old pernicious division between body and mind from which all of us have suffered for so long. There are many women like me who are Christians and Jews. The religious heritage of the West is our spiritual language. It provides our identity and tradition and gives us the communal symbols and idioms that enable us to

communicate our spiritual experiences and to learn from each other and from the generations before us. This is the framework in which we find our spiritual inspiration. We cannot seek the spiritual significance of the female aspects of our lives without centering that search in our Judeo-Christian heritage.

Where there is silence in the texts, we must act to fill that silence. We need to recover and transform our religious heritage to extend the images and concepts of our religions to incorporate our lives as individual embodied women. But our religious texts—androcentric and incomplete as they are—are the repositories of our cultural memory. They confront us with our past, and we cannot ignore them. If we hold on to them, they will change in our grasp, like Proteus, until eventually they tell us what we want to know. If we keep wrestling with the divine all night, as Jacob did, it will give us its blessing.[20]

Like Frymer-Kensky, Terry, Vered, Simha, and the other women of *A Weave of Women* speak of God, and "name towards God,"[21] out of both their experience and their tradition. Their voices "act to fill that silence" left by women's absence from the foundational texts of their faith. The women of *Weave* understand themselves to be Jews, and the God they worship is the one true God of Exodus and Sinai. If we hear Terry's prayer, addressed, "O God of women" as being directed at someone other than Yahweh, we will have fundamentally misunderstood not only her words but her entire community's experience of the divine. As readers, we need to recognize that not only is the novel as a whole a midrash on the book of Exodus, but the prayers and stories within the text are midrashic as well: that is, the women of *Weave* are bringing their own experience to ancient texts, and speaking new prayers and stories in the expectation that the reality behind the texts is wide enough to incorporate that experience.

The Character of God

We turn now to an analysis of the qualities of character expressed by or imputed to God in *A Weave of Women* and in Exodus. Aristotle insists that character is expressed through choice, "what sort of thing a man chooses or avoids in circumstances where the choice is not obvious."[22] In Exodus we have ample opportunity to witness God's actions, and thus God's choices: we see, for example, that God chooses to listen to the poor, not the powerful (see Exod. 3:7–8). In *Weave*, however, God does not appear as a character outright; rather, we gather our knowledge of God from the description offered to us by the women, usually in their prayer, of God's actions (choices) in their lives and experience. We will first look at God as portrayed in Exodus, and then turn to the much different portrayal presented in *A Weave of Women*.

God as Righteous Warrior

God's first action described by the book of Exodus is to approve the deceptive practices and words of the Israelite midwives, and to reward them for their actions. God's choice here indicates that the lives of children are more important to him than obedience to (human) authority, and that his approval merits concrete consequences. Both issues are significant: we gain both a sense of God's priorities, and of the extent of God's involvement in human affairs. That involvement is made more clear as the slavery of the Israelites increases in severity:

> The Israelites groaned under their slavery, and cried out. Out of the slavery their cry for help rose up to God. God heard their groaning, and God remembered his covenant with Abraham, Isaac, and Jacob. God looked upon the Israelites, and God took notice of them. (Exod. 2:23–25)

Here we see that God pays attention to suffering, and God keeps his promises. Neither is inevitable; both are choices, and indicative of the character of God. God could have ignored the suffering as ultimately unimportant, or could have chosen to break his promise to men long dead. Instead, God chose to intervene directly in the world, and deliver the Israelites from slavery to the Egyptians. Here we have the choice that most clearly delineates the character of God, and indeed is a central theological claim of both Jews and Christians today: God chose to act in history to liberate God's people.

The wonderful picture of the faithful, compassionate divine liberator, however, is tempered when we recall other choices made by God in the book of Exodus: he chose to harden Pharaoh's heart in order to display greater and greater signs and wonders; he chose to afflict all of Egypt with ghastly plagues; and he chose to kill "every first-born in the land of Egypt, both human beings and animals" (see Exod. 4:21; 7–12; 12:12). The story makes it clear that these are God's choices, and thus—as before, when the qualities at issue were faithfulness and compassion—we must see the violence and indiscriminate destruction here as indicative of God's character. Certainly the Israelites did, as we can see in the Song of the Sea, as they celebrate the God they have come to know:

I will sing to the LORD, for he has triumphed gloriously;
horse and rider he has thrown into the sea.
The LORD is my strength and my might,
and he has become my salvation;
this is my God, and I will praise him,
my father's God, and I will exalt him.
The LORD is a warrior;
the LORD is his name.
Pharaoh's chariots and his army he cast into the sea;
his picked officers were sunk in the Red Sea.
The floods covered them;
they went down into the depths like a stone.
Your right hand, O LORD, glorious in power—
your right hand, O LORD, shattered the enemy.
In the greatness of your majesty you overthrew your adversaries;
you sent out your fury, it consumed them like stubble (Exod. 15:1–7).

The picture of God we gain in the book of Exodus, then, is of someone whose faithfulness is to be trusted but whose anger is to be feared; someone whose compassion is limited to a particular circle of people; and someone whose saving activity is performed on a grand scale, with enemies left "shattered" and the workings of nature overturned. Not surprisingly, the women of *A Weave of Women* experience God in a much different way.

God as Mother

The reader's first introduction to the God whose presence shapes the telling of *A Weave of Women* is through a prayer recited by Simha after the birth of her daughter, Hava:

I come into your house, O Mother God. You inclined your ear toward me, and I will whisper into it all the days of my life.

The cords of life and death encompassed me. From the hollow of the grave, from the cave of the mouth of birth I called. I knew happiness and anguish. You delivered my soul from death into birth, my eyes from tears, my feet from falling. I shall walk before You in the land of the living. (8)

Readers familiar with the psalms will see that this prayer resembles Psalm 116; it is, indeed, a reimagining of that psalm from the perspective of a woman who has just given birth. The first nine verses of the original psalm (the only part used by Simha) are as follows:

> I love the Lord, because he has heard my voice and my supplications.
> Because he inclined his ear to me, therefore I will call on him as long as I live.
> The snares of death encompassed me; the pangs of Sheol laid hold on me;
> I suffered distress and anguish.
> Then I called on the name of the Lord: "O Lord, I pray, save my life!"
> Gracious is the Lord, and righteous; our God is merciful.
> The Lord protects the simple; when I was brought low, he saved me.
> Return, O my soul, to your rest, for the Lord has dealt bountifully with you.
> For you have delivered my soul from death, my eyes from tears, my feet
>   from stumbling.
> I will walk before the Lord in the land of the living.

The prayer arises out of an interaction between Simha's experience of labor and delivery and the language offered to her by her tradition; her combination of the two reveals much about her understanding of herself in relation to God, and about her understanding of the activity of God in her life. First, Simha met God in her own experience: God is not just the liberator of her ancestors, celebrated for past actions, but the one who acted here and now in Simha's life to deliver her "soul from death into birth, [her] eyes from tears, [her] feet from falling" (8). This deliverance, however, is vastly different than that of Exodus: there is no enemy to defeat, no soldiers to drown, no slavery to escape. Unlike the relentless sorrow and suffering of slavery, the experience of labor is one of both "happiness and anguish;" one in which both life and death are powerful realities for the laboring woman. "The hollow of the grave" is linked to "the cave of the mouth of birth," and both are difficult, frightening, transformative places from which one calls upon God.

Secondly, Simha transformed a description of generalized human fear and despair into a many-layered description of the difficulty and agony of birth through her use of womb imagery. Simha speaks of the "cords of life and death," recalling the umbilical cord that gives life to a child but which may also strangle the child during the birth process. She then moves on to the rounded, empty-but-waiting-to-be-filled images of "hollow," "grave," "cave," and "mouth," all of which reflect the womb. Finally, God's action is to "deliver" her, just as she delivered her child. Simha's prayer speaks of life and death, fear and peace, suffering and deliverance in terms drawn from her own experience of labor, and thus succeeds not only in transforming an androcentric psalm into a gynocentric one, but also in

speaking of redemption in a maternal voice. As you recall from our discussion of *Beloved*, the "maternal voice" tends to speak of redemption in
terms of wholeness and inclusivity. To be redeemed is not to leave death
and suffering behind, but to find a way to speak toward (if not fully understand) the wholeness and goodness of a reality that includes both death
and life, fear and peace. That Simha's prayer *on becoming a mother* recalls
these issues is especially appropriate.

Thirdly, we have to attend to the name and character of God. Simha
addressed her prayer to "O Mother God," and describes an intimate relationship characterized first and foremost by physical closeness: Simha has
come into the house of God, and is close enough to whisper into God's ear.
The primary action of God celebrated by Simha is that of listening: "you
inclined your ear toward me, and I will whisper into it all the days of my
life." In Exodus, God heard the cries of the Israelite slaves and responded
with a violent intervention in history; in *A Weave of Women*, God bent
close to Simha to hear her whisper, and will remain close always. This
emphasis on presence and proximity instead of activity is new. Certainly
Simha refers to God's deliverance, but both the beginning and the end of
the prayer emphasize God's nearness: God is close enough to whisper to;
Simha has entered into the house of God, and Simha will walk with God
throughout her life. Interestingly, the initiative and activity of the prayer
alternates between God and Simha: I come into your house, you inclined
your ear, I called, you delivered, I shall walk. The understanding of God
here is not drawn from the gratitude and passivity of a slave liberated by
a powerful warrior, but instead pictures an intimate partnership, a respon-
sive relationship of deep togetherness.

God's choices in Simha's psalm are to accept and welcome Simha's
presence in her house (she inclined her ear), to listen carefully to Simha's
soft words, to deliver her from suffering, and to walk with her always.
Welcoming and companionship are at the center of God's activity; there
are no enemies in this picture, and no violence. God's compassion and
faithfulness are directed at Simha, but not described as being limited to her.

Being close to God is a continuing theme. Like Simha, Vered adopts
one of the psalms when called upon to offer a prayer of thanksgiving and
celebration, and she, too, chooses one that emphasizes the presence and
nearness of God. Vered, a social worker, "recites the fifteenth Psalm of
David, but in the voice of Vered" (207) as a blessing on the new home for
runaway girls:

O, my Shehena, who shall live in your tent? Who shall dwell in the
Carmel? She that is upright and proud, that worketh righteousness and

speaks truth . . . speaks no ill with her tongue, does no evil to her sister. . . .
She that doeth thus shall never be moved from this dwelling. (207)

As is evident, too, in the metaphors used in Simha's psalm, Vered's
understanding of God grows out of her understanding of her own situation. Vered's understanding of what it means to be a righteous woman is
at the center of this psalm: her concern is to identify those who will live in
the company of God, and she claims that the one who does justice is the
one who dwells with the Holy. In her choice of pronouns, Vered names the
one who does justice as specifically female, a daring change yet one that
speaks directly to her audience of women and girls. Another interesting
alteration she makes in the original psalm is her initial description of the
one who shall dwell with God: "she that is upright and proud" has little
correspondence with Psalm 15, which describes "those who walk blame-
lessly" (Ps. 15:2). To claim pride and uprightness of carriage as indicative
of right behavior for women is unusual, especially given cultural assumptions that a woman who walks with eyes downcast in modesty is more to
be honored than one who looks boldly before her. Similarly, our culture
often sees pride as just another name for sinful self-presumption; to claim
it here as an element of what it means to be a righteous woman is a radical redefinition of both womanhood and righteousness.

The focus of the psalm again, like Simha's, is not nearly so much on
God's activity as on God's presence. Furthermore, the activity described
here is human, not divine. Vered is concerned with who is able to be with
God: who will dwell with God, who shall live in God's tent. The way to
know and experience God's presence is through right action; those who
act properly will always be in the presence of God, no matter what happens. Moreover, Vered's understanding of God's character is revealed in
the choices God is assumed to make: God is the one who chooses to be
present to the righteous, and who never abandons them.

Another significant issue is Vered's name for God. "O, my Shehena,"
she begins, instead of "O, Lord." Shehena, now more commonly spelled
Shekhinah, is the "indwelling presence of God" of the Jewish mystical tradition, and is commonly thought of in female or feminine terms, including
"princess, daughter, queen, mother, matron, moon, sea, faith, wisdom,
community of Israel, [and] mother Rachel."[23] To name God as "Shehena"
then, is to insist on mutuality and intimacy; indeed, as Broner has pointed
out in another context, "etymologically, *shikoon* is neighborhood. *Shekena*
[*Shehena; Shekhinah*] is a neighbor. We could nicely use such a neighborly
presence as She Who Dwells in Our Midst."[24] Vered's choice of a name for
God in this particular psalm thus offers the reader a clever play on words:

the psalm focuses on who shall dwell with God, and Vered names God as one who dwells with us.

Another issue raised by the idea of God's mutuality and intimacy is the nature of God's power. The "nonhierarchical" God who does not dominate suggests that God's power might not be the "power over" we so often imagine, but a "power with" that enables instead of dominates. Indeed, Judith Plaskow has suggested that the central issue in language about God is our understanding of the power of God.[25] If we understand God's power not as dominance but as a mutual, co-creative power that "elicits our power, meeting us in the shifting and changing forms of our lives,"[26] this would point to an image of partnership with God (also suggested in Simha's psalm). Such an understanding of God's power (and human power) would hint of more human responsibility in the world, as is only appropriate, especially within the Jewish tradition, given "the human accountability and effort that the covenant demands."[27]

The use of blessings in *A Weave of Women* also engages the issue of the name and thus the character of God. Blessings are a significant form of prayer in Judaism: there are blessings to recite before performing a *mitzvah*, or commandment; blessings recited before everyday events or pleasures (eating, drinking, wearing new clothing); and blessings recited at special times and events (such as a holiday, or upon seeing or doing something unusual). The blessings follow a formula, with each blessing beginning, "*Barukh atah adonay eloheynu melekh ha-olam*," traditionally translated as, "Blessed art thou, Lord our God, King of the Universe."[28] The blessings in *A Weave of Women* alter this time-honored formula, and name God not as the King of the Universe, but as "Mother of the Universe" (257) and "God of women." (207). The power of renaming the distant King and Lord as mother is extraordinary: it implies an entirely different relationship between the human and divine.

Two ancient, traditional Jewish blessings are featured in *A Weave of Women*—though of course, in altered form. The first is the blessing said when one affixes a mezuzah to the doorpost of a home. The mezuzah—a small cylinder containing a parchment inscribed with several verses of Deuteronomy—is both a sign of God's presence and a statement of the home's Jewishness, serving much the same purpose as, for example, a crucifix in a Catholic home. The second traditional blessing is the *sheheheyanu*, a blessing chanted to commemorate significant first events. The traditional mezuzah blessing and Terry's revision of it are as follows:

> Blessed are you, Lord, our God, King of the Universe, who has sanctified us with His commandments and commanded us to affix a mezuzah.

O God of Women, Thou hast made us holy by Thy commandments and commanded us to affix a mezuzah. This designates a righteous house of women. (207)

The first thing to notice, of course, is that God is named "God of Women." While this can be read as exclusionary (the God of women, not the God of men), I believe that instead it needs to be seen as a particular, but not exclusive, name for God. The God of Abraham, we know, is not the God of Abraham alone; when we name God the Lord of the Sea that does not imply that someone else is Lord of the Fields and Forests. Especially given the context—the fulfillment of a commandment given by Yahweh—it makes sense to assume that this is a name not for a god (goddess?) who cares only for women, but for God who is here *explicitly named as caring for women*. That is the point: the one true God *is* the God of women, cares for them, and has made them holy. Further, God has made them holy through the gift of commandments: the women have duties to fulfill, and in affixing the mezuzah, they are responding to God and fulfilling their duties. They are not passive but active in their relationship with the divine.

The mezuzah is, of course, a reminder of God's presence. God is named in this prayer as the one who gave the commandments and the one who made the people holy, but God is also understood as the one whose presence and love are so real as to mark one's hands, heart, head, and home. The mezuzah, containing fifteen verses from Deuteronomy reminding Israel of God's blessings and the importance of keeping God's commandments, "is a constant reminder of God's presence. It functions as a visible sign that the home is Jewish, that the lives of those who live there should be marked by the love of God and the values that such love implies."[29] Like the two psalms discussed earlier, then, the choice of this particular blessing focuses our attention on the women's experience of God as present in their lives.

The other blessing spoken in *A Weave of Women* is the *sheheheyanu*. Its traditional form, followed by Simha's alteration of it, are as follows:

Blessed are you, Lord, our God, King of the Universe, who has kept us alive, sustained us, and enabled us to reach this season.

Blessed art thou, O Mother of the Universe, from whose body we descend, who has kept us alive, preserved us and brought us to this time, this season. (257)

While the change from "King of the Universe" to "Mother of the Universe" is significant, it is the addition of the phrase "from whose body we descend" that marks this prayer as bearing a much different understanding of God than tradition has dictated. For here God is not only named as mother, but given a body—a female body. Simha recites the prayer to inaugurate a new holiday, Holy Body Day, celebrated by the women to honor their bodies and to recover from the physical assaults so many of them have endured. Given the nature of this holiday, the conventional notion of God as pure spirit, separate from matter, is inappropriate. However, rather than assuming that the women here are simply heading "too far" in the other direction, and have in fact chosen to speak of God in a way reminiscent of pagan Greek tales of gods siring human (or half-human) children, I would like to explore another possibility. Sallie McFague, in *The Body of God*, introduces a new way to think about the traditionally opposed categories of body and spirit: we are not spirits locked in clay prisons but "inspirited bodies."[30] An inspirited body is first and foremost a body, and it is one given life by the spirit breathing within it. Actually, this is not an especially new way to think about human beings, and it could be argued that it is in fact a more biblical way than our more common notion that the true essence of a person is the "soul," with the body no more than a troublesome container to be shed at death. Remember the creation of Adam? "The Lord God formed man from the dust of the ground, and breathed into his nostrils the breath of life; and man became a living being" (Gen. 2:7) The living being—the human—is a body that breathes, not a soul wearing an overcoat. In the creation of Holy Body Day, and in the use of a prayer that connects God's breath to our bodies (our selves), the women of *A Weave of Women* are insisting that God is not separate from their bodies and their concerns; indeed, God is always and everywhere in the midst of them.

The portrait of God that emerges from the prayers and blessings spoken by Terry, Simha, and the other women of *A Weave of Women* is that of a mother who cares for them, who is present to them in their bodies (and in physical acts such as giving birth) and their behavior (fulfilling the commandments, acting in a way that is righteous). Interestingly, God is often seen more as a partner than as a provider: the women respond to God not only with praise and thanksgiving, but with creativity and action of their own. Like the portrait of God in Exodus, God here is compassionate, faithful, and loves justice. The difference lies primarily in the women's failure to identify an enemy for God to destroy: this is made clear in the creation of Holy Body Day, where the women who have been raped and beaten do not ask God to shatter their enemies and cast them into the sea, but instead pray in thanksgiving to the God who gave them their bodies, who is with them in their physical existence, and who "has kept us alive, preserved us and brought us to this time, this season." With this new understanding of God in mind, we turn now to the ending of the story, to see how the saving activity of God who is Mother and *Shekhinah* affects the plot of Broner's midrash.

Shekhinah and Exodus

While a well-constructed plot connects one incident logically to the next, the logic of the connections is not limited to mere causation, in the sense that any given action has certain logical consequences. Rather, character and theme are at issue, too, in a plot's construction of how events are grasped together as a whole. The causal sequence of events in *A Weave of Women* seems to pull the story out of the realm of midrash, but this is true only if we neglect how a plot is formed by the actions of its main character. Now that we have seen the true character of God in *Weave*, we can see that this, in combination with the end of the novel, offers us the clues necessary to understand the true trajectory set up in the beginning and middle of the novel: the presence of God and the joy of the women emphasized in the end make their seeming abandonment by God in the middle no more than a misreading prompted by our traditional expectations about the character and activity of God. We were looking for the God familiar to us from Exodus; when we didn't see enemies shattered and vengeance poured out on the wicked, we assumed that God must be absent. But it wasn't God who was missing, it was a particular (male) experience of God as a warrior instead of a mother. In order to demonstrate this, we first need to look at the novel's ending, and then return to its middle, to a second consideration of Hava's death. We will see that God's presence is indeed a constant in the story, even at its shattered center. We already know that God's presence was evident in the beginning of the story, for Simha's psalm described the presence of God in her labor and Hava's birth. Once we revisit Hava's death, we will see that the women's exodus is grounded in the presence of God that has always been a part of their lives; it is not, as it seemed before, an unworkable surprise ending that does not fit the plot of the story.

The exodus event at the end of *A Weave of Women* is made possible through the presence of God, and powerfully displays not only the all-enveloping character of that presence, but also the women's joy in it. The first thing to notice about this exodus is that it is a birth: just as in Exodus, in which a nation was born, so, too, in *Weave* a new society is born. Moreover, the beginning of this new society is described in terms that are drawn explicitly from the experience of childbirth: the women squat in preparation for their large deed, and the deed itself is described as squatting in an abandoned village. Squatting is a traditional posture for a birthing woman, long ignored in the West where a doctor's convenience outweighed the mother's comfort, but recently returning to the notice of women and their birth attendants. It is a posture favored both because it opens the pelvis (making delivery easier) and because it affords the laboring woman a measure of comfort and control not available to her if she is lying down. Because the squatting here not only suggests but is explicitly linked to giving birth, the reader recalls the birth of Hava, and thus Simha's psalm invoking the presence of God in labor and delivery. God is again present to the women in "the cave of the mouth of birth," although this is the birth of a commune, not a child, and again delivers them "from death into birth."

The next issue of importance in the exodus of the women is that the presence of God is indicated by the constant references to the women's enmeshment in biblical realities. The exodus is in fact made possible by the women's presence in the land of Israel, the land where God's presence is inescapable. The power and the promise of The Land (and by extension, the God of this Land) is made real through the bodily experience of the women, in the foods they eat: "The daughters of Jerusalem eat the biblical foods of The Land: the grape, honey, fig, date, pomegranate, almond" (286). They are living very much within the bounds of biblical reality, and the basic reality of the Bible is the presence and care of God.

Simha's wedding, which takes place immediately after the women's exodus from Jerusalem, makes the presence and care of God in the women's lives even more obvious. While ritual was always an important part of the women's lives, this is the first ritual whose specifically Jewish nature is emphasized and celebrated: Simha prepares for the wedding with a ritual bath, or *mikveh*; the wedding party blows the shofar; the couple is married under a huppah; and Simha wears a tallith, a prayer shawl that had belonged to Hepzibah's late father. The kibbutznik refuses to wear it because he is an atheist; the clear implication of Simha's wearing of the shawl is that she is not.

God, then, is clearly present throughout the women's exodus and their celebrations afterwards; we now need to seek the ways in which God is also present when Hava is mourned. Simha's grief at Hava's death is terrible, intense, and beyond reason, yet it is certainly not beyond the bounds of what might be expected and accepted from a mother who has lost a child. She wails; she mourns; she lays her body across the earth that encloses her daughter's body (134). "I am a stone," she says (134), leaving both life and death behind as she claims the status of inanimate matter. "I do not accept this," she insists. "Neither death nor life" (135). This refusal to accept either death (Hava's) or life (her own) is marked by a refusal to re-enter her home after Hava's funeral, and her refusal to "sleep or eat or attend services. She sits on her hard chair, feverish from her engorged breasts . . . she cannot pray and will not entreat" (135). It is under these circumstances that Terry's strange pronouncement, "we must make a firmament between heaven and earth . . . between reality and unreality," (139) must be understood. For Simha in her grief has left the realm of God's good creation; she must somehow be brought back. Like the earth before creation—without form and void—so, too, is Simha's life, without the structure of ritual, the peace of sleep, and the renewal of eating. Terry's pronouncement is not a usurpation of God's powers, but an acknowledgment of them: the women live within God's creation, and that fact must somehow be brought home to Simha, who has refused it in favor of an existence (not life) marked only by the chaos and darkness of grief.

The women's re-creation of reality for Simha takes place at the sea, "for some reason," Terry says (139), either not stating or not realizing that the sea is a familiar image of the *Shekhinah*. Simha's sudden desire to go to the *yam*, the sea, can thus be seen either as her own desire to return to life and God, or as God's pull on her, God's refusal to abandon her to life-negating grief. Simha's cry of greeting to the sea is revealing: "*Yam, yam*," Simha cries, "I didn't see you for such a long time!" (141) And it is certainly true that Simha has not seen the sea, nor her God, for a long time; but the sea was always present, and by implication, so was God. Moreover, Simha's move from stone-like, frozen grief to active mourning enables her to identify with another familiar image of the *Shekhinah*, who is known not only as Mother but as Mother Rachel, whose voice is raised in "lamentation and bitter weeping. Rachel is weeping for her children; she refuses to be comforted for her children, because they are no more" (Jer. 31:15).

The mourning ritual devised at the sea by Simha's friends focuses on acceptance: acceptance of salt, change, mystery, departures, moorings, flights, and even the acceptance of being broken in half. Each of these things (and several more) are symbolized by something found at the sea or on the shore: the saltiness of the water, the changing nature of waves, the flight of gulls, and a shell broken in two. Simha's acceptance of her status as a bereft mother is framed as an acceptance of creation and of her place in it: all these things of the sea live in the embrace of the sea/*Shekhinah*, and Simha, too, now accepts life in that embrace. The presence of God in Simha's life is made manifest both in the complex reality of the sea (in its salt, waves, sounds, as aspects of creation) and in the form of her friends.

The ritual of mourning and rebirth ends with Terry's instruction, "Accept support. Sit in the crotch of a tree, lean against a branch or accept an embrace. [Say,] 'I accept firm support in my life and in our friendship'" (144). Simha, who had refused support and refused life until her journey to the sea, now "clings to Terry, then to the kibbutznik" (144). In the end, she is able to accept not only the emotional support offered by her friends, but the physical support her body needs in order to survive: "That night, in the early hours, on the last day of mourning, the kibbutznik, the cowherd, milks Simha" (144). Simha's breasts, engorged with milk, were not only painful but a potential source of infection, and she had already been described as "feverish" because of them (135). The act of releasing the milk not only relieved her pain but quite probably saved her from serious illness (mastitis). Her acceptance of this aid marks her return to life; her friends have created for her "a firmament between heaven and earth," and once again she dwells in the land of the living.

We can see now that the plot of the novel can be summarized, like that of Exodus, in terms of God's actions: God is with Simha in labor; God is with Simha in her grief; God is with Simha in her joy. As with Exodus, the emphasis is on God as the primary character in the story, but *A Weave of Women* focuses on God's *presence*: God's primary, necessary, and salvific activity is simply to dwell with Simha and the other women. Moreover, the *joy* presented here as a necessary part of living in the presence of God corresponds to the joy celebrated in Exodus at the Song of the Sea. Despite the complexity inherent in re-creating plot, character, and action through the machinations of midrashic imagination, we have seen that in *Weave*, the God of Exodus—now understood as the *Shekhinah*—is a God who saves. More importantly, we have seen Broner succeed in healing our imaginations through the telling of a story that is both old and new. She has opened the door for us to embrace a new understanding of God by transforming a familiar story about God; our hearts, not just our minds, now see both God and the Exodus in a powerful new way. The "motherly" understanding of redemption that we began to glimpse through Sethe and the other mothers of *Beloved* is becoming more concrete, more real as we consider Broner's tale of God's powerful, living presence.

Our journey has been fruitful so far, yet it is not finished. Recall that we wanted to explore the stories women told about themselves, God, and the world before returning to stories of Jesus. We have accomplished much in our examination of the first two, and now we must turn to the third. There are, of course, many ways to talk about what the world is like, but I have chosen to focus on one aspect of our lives: our existence in time. Time is a more troublesome concept than you might imagine, and considering it helps us think about concepts as varied as our place in history, how story-telling works, and how we construct meaning in our lives. Barbara Kingsolver will be our guide for this difficult yet fascinating part of our travels, through her time-shifting novel, *Animal Dreams*.

Notes

1. Valerie Saiving, "The Human Situation: A Feminine View," in *The Journal of Religion* (April 1960). Reprinted in Carol Christ and Judith Plaskow, eds., *Womanspirit Rising: A Feminist Reader in Religion* (San Francisco: HarperSanFrancisco, 1992; originally published 1979), 25–42.

2. E. M. Broner, *A Weave of Women* (Bloomington: Indiana University Press, 1985. Originally published by Holt, Rinehart, and Winston, 1978.)

3. Elizabeth Johnson, *She Who Is: The Mystery of God in Feminist Theological Discourse* (New York: Crossroad, 1992), 85, 86.

4. Ibid., 95.

5. Judith Plaskow, *Standing Again at Sinai: Judaism from a Feminist Perspective* (San Francisco: Harper & Row, 1990), 1.

6. See Aristotle, *The Poetics*, Loeb Classical Library (Cambridge, MA: Harvard University Press, 1982; originally published 1927).

7. Ibid., 39.

8. Michael Walzer, *Exodus and Revolution* (New York: Basic Books, 1985), 5.

9. Ibid., 10–11.

10. Marc Gellman, *Does God Have a Big Toe? Stories about Stories in the Bible* (New York: Harper & Row, 1989), vii.

11. Howard Schwartz, *Reimagining the Bible: The Storytelling of the Rabbis* (New York: Oxford, 1998), 3.

12. Ibid., 11.

13. Judith Plaskow, "Jewish Memory from a Feminist Perspective," in *Weaving the Visions: New Patterns in Feminist Spirituality*, ed. Judith Plaskow and Carol P. Christ (San Francisco: Harper & Row, 1989), 46.

14. Sandra Schneiders, "The Bible and Feminism: Biblical Theology," in *Freeing Theology: The Essentials of Theology in Feminist Perspective*, ed. Catherine Mowry LaCugna (San Francisco: HarperSanFrancisco, 1993), 34.

15. Ibid., 36.

16. Ibid.

17. Plaskow, *Standing Again at Sinai*, xx.

18. Ibid., 29.

19. Rosemary Radford Ruether, *Sexism and God-Talk: Toward a Feminist Theology* (Boston: Beacon Press, 1983), 18.

20. Tikva Frymer-Kensky, *Motherprayer: The Pregnant Woman's Spiritual Companion* (New York: G. P. Putnam Sons, 1995), xvii–xviii.

21. Plaskow, *Standing Again at Sinai*, 154–55.

22. Aristotle, *The Poetics*, 29.

23. Plaskow, *Standing Again at Sinai*, 138.

24. E.M. Broner, *The Telling: The Story of a Group of Jewish Women who Journey to Spirituality through Community and Ceremony* (San Francisco: HarperSanFrancisco, 1993), 2.

25. Plaskow, *Standing Again at Sinai*, 128.

26. Ibid., 140.

27. Ibid., 133.

28. Ibid., 142.

29. Morris Kertzer, *What is a Jew?*, rev. ed. Lawrence A. Hoffman (New York: Collier, 1993), 171.

30. Sallie McFague, *The Body of God: An Ecological Theology* (Minneapolis: Fortress Press, 1993), 20.

Chapter 4

TIME AND THE TELLING OF STORIES
Redemption in *Animal Dreams*

We have reached a difficult point in our journey. Up until now, we have considered essentially concrete ideas—sometimes complex, but always solid and graspable. The history of the idea of redemption, suffering, and the work of mothers, the Exodus story: all these things are, in some sense, relatively straightforward. But our consideration of *Animal Dreams* will be different.[1] We are about to plunge into a theoretical discussion of the workings of time, something that is no small philosophical problem. Yet it is a crucial discussion for us, as our understanding of time grounds our understanding of how and why we tell stories, and more importantly, how and why redemption is even possible.

Time—both its existence and the way we expect it to behave—is such a fundamental part of the way we tell stories that we rarely stop to examine our assumptions about it. This, of course, is a problem, because our *assumptions* about time and the *truth* about time are two very different things. Indeed, our common sense understanding of what time is and how it works leads us into theological difficulties so serious we usually prefer not to think about them. For example, time, as we understand it, would not seem to permit redemption to take place at all. We see time as heading only in one direction—from the past, through the present, and on into the future—and so the past is lost to us forever. But if the past is gone, then gone, too, is any chance of redeeming, in any meaningful way, the suffering that took place in the past. As Christians, we hold the conviction that the redemption of suffering is and must be more than a belated consolation or "pie in the sky by and by," and so we need to figure out how to deal with the troubling fact that we cannot go back in time to right wrongs. Theologian Marjorie Suchocki points out that true justice, like true redemption, would have to mean "the redress of evil and the restoration of well-being to those for whom it has been violated or lost," but laments that such a justice can never be achieved:

> Too often injustice has crushed its victims, making reparation impossible. How is a broken mind repaired, a lost limb returned, a stunted ability to love reshaped, a murder undone? . . . The more one begins to consider the problem of justice, the more impossible and visionary any full justice appears to be. . . . Only if the past can somehow be brought into the present, and only if a sufficient flexibility of vision can allow radical diversities to co-exist in well-being, only then can justice in its fullest dimensions be established. Under the circumstances of our finitude, however, such conditions cannot be secured.[2]

Although Suchocki's concern here is justice, not redemption, the problem remains the same: how are terrible wrongs righted? How can injustice be undone? How can suffering be not only healed but redeemed (made whole)? She not only identifies the problem in clear, even shocking terms (how *is* a broken mind repaired?) and declares it impossible to solve, she also identifies the key aspect of the problem that makes it unsolvable: time. "Only if the past can somehow be brought into the present," she declares, and then dismisses that as impossible "under the circumstances of our finitude" (75). Given our typical understanding of time, she is absolutely right. However, we also believe that redemption is real, and available to us here and now. How are we to make sense of this contradiction? We are boxed in by the limitations inherent in the story we tell about time and how it works, even as our hope and our experience (of healing, of wholeness, of redeeming love) tell us that redemption is possible.

Clearly we need to take a good look at the story we tell about time: what it is, how it works, and how our lives are shaped by it. You might be surprised to hear that philosophers have struggled with these questions for centuries; after all, anyone with a working watch knows what time it is. Yet there has been endless philosophical puzzling about what time is, exactly, and what it measures and how that measurement is accomplished. What does time measure? Well, the passage of time, of course! The passage of *what*? Well, the passage of the sun through the sky, perhaps. So does time pass at night? Yes, so perhaps one could define time as measuring the space (?) or distance (?) between noon on one day and noon on the next. But how do you define "noon" without a watch? If you say, "When the sun is directly overhead," then you run into the problem that days aren't exactly 24 hours long, nor years exactly 365 days. But how did we determine that? The history of exact measurement of time is complex and fascinating, but not exactly what we're after here. I just wanted you to realize that, like St. Augustine, we are left saying, "What then, is time? I know well enough what it is, provided nobody asks me; but if I am asked what it is and try to explain, I am baffled."[3]

In order to sort through some of the theological difficulties raised by this tricky thing called time, I would like to plot out carefully the strange workings of time in Barbara Kingsolver's *Animal Dreams*, a novel whose main focus is the suffering and redemption of a woman named Codi Noline. In Codi's story, we not only see how time plays a part in redemption, but also, as readers, we are forced to experience time in a new way due to the ways in which the novel is constructed. This does two linked and very powerful things: first, it solves our theological problem about time and redemption. Second, it demonstrates that the narrative aspect of our experience is central to our understanding of the wholeness of things and therefore of redemption. What do I mean by "the narrative aspect of our experience"? Simply this: we understand our lives—our experiences— by constructing stories. We do not experience any given day of our lives as a series of completely random sensory events with no history nor future, but instead see these events as part of the ongoing story of our life, which meshes with the stories of other people's lives, and the story of our country and our faith community and many other things. We gather together the fragments that make up our day, and see them as part of many ongoing stories—such as the one about how you and your sister have never really gotten along since she moved away, or the one about your crazy boss, or the one about your marriage, or the one about your fear of flying. We understand the events in our lives by putting them in context, and as human beings, we give things context by telling the story of the history that led to a given event. No given experience stands alone: we incorporate into the way we understand our lives by incorporating it into a story. This is what I mean by the "narrative aspect of our experience."

We can see fairly easily that the idea of redemption is what we might call a "narrative concept," that is, an idea that tells a story. In this case, redemption is a concept that includes some kind of story of original wholeness, then brokenness, then restored wholeness. However, to claim that the narrative aspect of our experience is central to our understanding of redemption is more than the simple, definitional claim that redemption is a narrative concept. Instead, it is a much broader claim that *it is only through the telling of stories that redemption can happen at all*. Redemption, in other words, is not simply a matter of the cross but of the stories we tell about the cross. This is why, in the next chapter, we will be looking at the stories Jesus told us, and especially at the stories that we tell each other *about* Jesus in the Gospels. The stories we tell about Jesus really matter! If we tell the wrong stories, the redemption that Jesus offered us gets lost: we no longer know what it is, nor how to reach it. Before we turn to those important discussions, however, we must first explore the idea that Kingsolver's novel can provide us with an understanding of time that enables us to make sense of redemption.

Redemption, if it is to include justice and the restoration of wrongs, requires that the past be open to change and renewal. In other words, redemption requires that the future can change the past. This may sound impossible to us, but in *Animal Dreams*, Barbara Kingsolver shows us the gaps and slippages where time is indeed open, and where history is not as fixed as we assume. Many novels play with the idea of time, but too often those that do, do it in such a difficult way that very few people are able to read the book with any sort of interest or comprehension. For example, if you've ever read a novel in which "stream of consciousness" narration is used, or if you have ever tackled James Joyce's great but immensely difficult novel *Ulysses*, you'll know what I mean. Too often this kind of experimentation is for English professors only: not many of us have the time or energy to fight our way through such unfamiliar, unmarked territory. The genius of Kingsolver's novel is that it is perfectly readable, even inviting, and yet still manages to offer us a new understanding of time and how time works in our lives. This novel does not disorient us with strange, experimental narrative techniques that challenge our everyday experience; rather, it deploys our everyday experience in such a way that it becomes clear that what we experience does not match up with what we say we believe, and *what we experience is more true than what we believe.*

Finally, this issue of time and redemption is of particular interest to women. More than men, women have suffered from our traditional Western understanding that time is linear and progressive. Ancient peoples understood time through the analogy of the seasons: they repeated themselves every year. Time, then, was cyclical; it did not move on permanently, but always returned to the beginning, over and over. However, once time is understood as linear rather than cyclical—as relentlessly moving on rather than renewing itself endlessly—then human existence within time becomes terrifyingly limited, with death seen as a permanent end point rather than one aspect of a continual cycle of death and new life. The religious implications of this were striking: women, once images of fertility and renewal, came to be seen as the source of a bodily existence that was finite, corruptible, and ultimately inhuman. Women and their capability to give birth became, oddly, symbols of death, rather than signs of hope and new life. Fortunately, the idea of linear time, like cyclical, is not "the truth" about time. It is just an idea, a human construct meant to make sense of our experience. If our experience does not conform to its theory, then it is useless. Kingsolver's novel suggests that there is more to the truth about time than the story we tell about its linear nature. Rather, she portrays a time that is open and flexible in surprising ways—ways that will help us to understand better how redemption is possible, and how women participate in the new life it offers us.

Constructing the Story, Reconstructing Time

Throughout *Animal Dreams*, Barbara Kingsolver challenges our assumptions about time. She does this in the way she tells the story, in its setting, and in its themes. Each of these aspects of the novel—its structure, narration, setting, and themes—needs to be examined in detail in order to see how brilliantly and how deeply Kingsolver is challenging us to see in a new way. Now, it is entirely possible that you have never picked apart the way a novel is put together with the kind of thoroughness that I will ask you to follow over the rest of this chapter, but believe me, such attention to detail will pay off. Writers are not fools and their job is not easy: they put together stories with the same care and precision that engineers use in building suspension bridges, or chefs use in preparing elegant meals. If we open our eyes to the serious work Barbara Kingsolver put into making this story flow effortlessly across several decades and several narrators, we will be wonderfully rewarded.

Our first task is to look at the *structure* of the novel. Some of the questions we might ask include: How is the story put together? Does she start at point A and tell everything in order from the beginning to the end? Are there chapter divisions, or does everything flow together? How many people tell this story? Are the narrators trustworthy? Some stories spring great surprises in the end when it turns out that the narrator was deliberately lying, or half-consciously shading the truth, or simply ignoring crucial things. You may well ask, why are all these issues important to us? The answer is simple: the way we structure stories and the way we understand time are intimately related. In his famous three-volume study, *Time and Narrative*, philosopher and literary critic Paul Ricoeur argues that it is through the construction of narrative plots that we make sense of the chaos of our lives.[4] The many individual events of our days, years, and entire lives are random and chaotic, until we construct a story through which to understand them. Reconfiguring the chaos of daily life through storytelling is a human necessity: we can't live without it! Chaos silences us; while it may be reality, it is impossible to grasp. It is only through *emplotment*, the process of ordering and structuring our experience—grasping things together, as Ricoeur says[5]—that we are able to put words to what we have experienced, and thereby to give it sense and meaning. A carefully plotted novel, then—one whose structure is architecturally sound, with no staircases to nowhere nor rooms left unroofed—is both something other than our experience of time, and the best way we have of understanding that experience, because we can only deal with time when we have captured its movement in a story. As Ricoeur says, "time becomes human time to the extent that it is organized after the manner of a narrative; narrative, in turn, is meaningful to the extent that it portrays the features of temporal experience."[6] And *Animal Dreams* portrays the features of temporal experience—or shows us how time works—in ways that help us understand this difficult concept in new and powerful ways.

The seemingly straightforward telling of *Animal Dreams* conceals a cunningly plotted and organized novel. Barbara Kingsolver uses several narrative devices to construct not only her plot but time itself in her story. First, she sets up clear boundaries by using formal structural devices such as a table of contents and named chapters. Secondly, she uses three different first-person narrators, all of whom have some sort of trouble with time, to keep the reader off-balance, yet not hopelessly so since the boundaries remain as anchor points. Finally, there is the organizational key to the book, the Mexican and Mexican-American holiday of the Day of the Dead. Kingsolver uses this holiday to propose an entirely different model of the relationship between past and present than we have come to understand in our rational, linear, "common sense" understanding of time.

Setting the Boundaries: A Formal Structure

Kingsolver's use of a table of contents and named chapters suggests to us from the beginning that *Animal Dreams* has more in common with the familiar, safe, realistic novels most of us read than with the difficult, chaotic, experimental works that make bold philosophical pronouncements about time and other "big" issues through their very style and structure. Yet this is somewhat misleading. Kingsolver's narrative is neither as familiar nor as safe as we might at first assume. The obvious formal structuring is not a sign of an old-fashioned, straightforward story, but instead works to set up limits within which she, too, can experiment with bold philosophical ideas yet in a way we can follow. Think of the carefully defined parameters of a laboratory experiment: within these fixed boundaries, new, yet controlled, things can happen.

While most novels today are divided into chapters, not all of them have a table of contents. For many stories, it is sufficient to put a number in bold type at the top of a page to indicate a new chapter. Kingsolver chose instead to lay out a table of contents: she not only divided her story into chapters, she named them, and then listed them before the story begins so that we can get a glimpse of what is to come. The table of contents is divided into fourteen sections, each containing from one to six chapters. At first glance, we might not see any real structure beyond the alternation of sections between Cosima and Homero. The differing lengths of the sections, and the fact that Kingsolver hides the connection between the first, middle, and last chapters by altering the name of a single holiday, serve to obscure what turns out to be a very well-organized and designed structure. The sections are identified by the name of their narrator, either Cosima (Codi) or Homero (Doc Homer). The fact that the formal name rather than the familiar name of each narrator is used suggests again the precision and specificity of a laboratory experiment, and serves to create a certain distance between the structure of the story and its actual, more casual telling. Further, time becomes an issue even here, in the use of Doc Homer's formal name. When we begin to read the story, after all, we have no idea that Homer Noline was born and grew up as Homero Nolina. This fact is not revealed until close to the end of the novel, at which point his name as given in the table of contents suddenly makes sense. Learning that Doc Homer really is Homero transforms our understanding of what has come before: no longer are his section headings an unexplained oddity, but a sign of his true self. We now understand the early part of the novel in a new way, and understand Homer and Codi's past in a new way. This new understanding effectively alters the past for us as readers.

The table of contents not only sets up a structure for us to follow, it also marks out that structure by naming the narrator, or the one whose point of view we share for a given chapter. Each section of the novel is identified by its primary narrator, either Doc Homer or Codi. Doc Homer's chapters—always only a single chapter per section—are narrated in the third person, but clearly his are the eyes through which the reader sees and understands the action. Codi's much more extensive sections, ranging from one to six chapters, are told in the first person, and create an intimacy with the reader that makes the transition from her sections to her father's more distant ones jarring.

Shaking the Boundaries: Three Different Narrators

Perhaps the most interesting thing about Doc Homer's chapters is that it is easy to forget that they are there. *Animal Dreams* is so clearly Codi's story that it is surprising to realize that Doc Homer opens the novel, not Codi, and that it is his memories that drive the plot and explain much of what Codi (and we) fail to understand throughout the story. The fact that his sections are narrated in what literary critics call "an omniscient third-person voice" may account for some of this: the narrator reaches into Doc Homer's head and heart, but is clearly separate from him, and thus we never identify with him the way it is possible to identify with Codi. In the following passage, for example, the strict location of point-of-view with Homer alone is as clear as the narrator's distance from him. The reader sees only what Homer sees, but is removed from the experience:

> He turns his pillow and rests his head on it carefully because his brain gets jostled and things move around inside his head like olives in a jar of brine. Think about the flood. He is going south on the near side of the arroyo. He stops to look back upstream and his light finds them, by pure luck, on the opposite bank, Cosima's thin, waving arms shine like the crisscrossing blades of scissors. They are screaming but he only sees their mouths stretched open like the mouths of fledgling birds. . . How does he reach them? A boat? No, that wouldn't have been possible. He sits up again. He has no clear image of reaching them, no memory of their arms on his neck, he only hears them crying over the telephone. And then he understands painfully that he wasn't able to go to them. There is no memory because he wasn't there. He had to call Uda Dell on the other side of the arroyo. Her husband was alive then, and went down the bank on his mule to find them. (20)

This passage moves effortlessly between the past—Doc Homer's search for his girls in a flood—and the present, when he is trying to remember the flood after being awakened by a nightmare in which he relived his search. Interestingly, the narrator's account of the present and Doc Homer's memory of the past are both narrated in the present tense: "He turns his pillow [present] . . . He is going south [past] . . . He stops [past] . . ." This confusion of the past and present serves two functions: first, it reminds us that Doc Homer often cannot distinguish between the past and present. As a victim of Alzheimer's disease, his sense of time, memory, and the "present-ness" of events are highly suspect. Secondly and perhaps more interestingly, however, the narration of a memory in the present tense reminds us that memories do, to a certain extent, function in the present tense as we recall them. "So I'm walking down the street and this guy says to me" may not meet an English teacher's standards for narration of a past event, but the colloquial insistence on recasting the past into the present *as it is being told* is significant nonetheless. It is grammatically wrong because it gives a false impression of when things happened, but it points to our *experience* of memories as things which happen *now*, even if it is incontestably true that the event (not the memory) happened in the past.

Like her father, Codi also has trouble with the past and the present. Her problems, however, are not rooted in illness, but in forgetfulness. She has somehow forgotten most of her childhood, recognizing neither familiar faces nor places when she returns to Grace after an absence of fourteen years. Her narration of the present focuses extensively on the fact that she has no remembered background for it: events seem to be happening in a vacuum, even though she knows that a past and an understanding for them exist somehow (in other people's memories, if not her own). Interestingly, her narration of the present takes place in the past tense. Thus while Doc Homer conflates the past and present by narrating both in the present, Codi conflates them by narrating both in the past. In either case, sorting out what is happening now and what happened years before is not at all difficult for us as we read. This may seem surprising when we think about it, but there is no surprise nor difficulty while we are simply reading the story. In fact, it is only surprising because when we think about time, we assume that the past and present have to remain separate, yet when we simply think and live, we often experience both past and present at the same time, just like Codi and her father.

This experience of the fluidity of the past and present is both constructed by Kingsolver and lived/remembered by us as we read. In the novel, Kingsolver deliberately chooses verb tenses and patterns of storytelling that merge and mix the past and present (in different ways at different times), but the reader is not disoriented by this because it corresponds to our lived experience. However, it most emphatically does not correspond to the reader's "common sense" understanding of how time works, and Kingsolver's artificial construction of a common experience helps the reader recognize the significant gap between that experience and the "common sense" that purports to explain it. For if the past is lost to us, why does it make sense to tell the story of a memory in the present tense? And if we have no access to events that happened years ago, why does Doc Homer wake up with his heart pounding in fear because his young daughters— long since found and grown up—are lost? "His circulatory system believes they are still lost" (20) is the explanation Kingsolver provides, and the reader recognizes its truth: in our dreams, in our memories, *and in our bodies*, the past lives on.

Kingsolver uses still another narrative technique to prompt the reader to understand that the past is not as fixed and finished as we usually assume. Codi's fallible voice reminds the reader of the gap between memory and reality. "Memory is a complicated thing," Codi muses, "a relative to truth but not its twin" (48). Throughout the novel, Codi experiences her memory as untrustworthy, fragmented, and disruptive, but as Codi and the reader eventually learn, this is because what Codi "knows" about the past is often wrong. As an adolescent, she settled the conflict between what she remembered and what she knew to be true by deciding that her memories must be wrong, and thus denying/"forgetting" them; when she finally learned that it was her understanding of the past that was in error, her lost memories returned. As Viola explained to her at the end of the novel, "No, if you remember something, then it's true . . . In the long run, that's what you've got" (342).

Kingsolver makes it clear to the reader from the beginning that Codi's voice is fallible when speaking of the past. As narrator, Codi herself confesses to remembering what she has not seen, and failing to remember what she has (48). However, Codi's openness with us about her memory problems serves as a cover for the memory problems she neither confesses nor knows about. Throughout much of the story, we know that Codi cannot remember much of her childhood, but we accept—as Codi does—the memories that do exist. When Kingsolver reveals these memories to be false constructions, Codi's understanding of herself undergoes a radical shift, and the reader's understanding of Codi and of time itself undergoes a corresponding disruption. In the beginning, we assumed with Codi that the past was fixed but often unknowable; in the end, Codi's experience teaches us that *what is known changes what is real*. The most potent example of this comes at Hallie's funeral, when Codi realizes that the distant townswomen of her childhood were in fact all the mothers she never had:

> Doña Althea clumped forward with her cane and set down a miniature, perfectly made peacock piñata. . . it was for Hallie. I tried to listen to what she was saying. She said, "I made one like this for both of you girls, for your *cumpleaños* when you were ten."
>
> To my surprise, this was also true. I remembered every toy, every birthday party, each one of these fifty mothers who'd been standing at the edges of my childhood, ready to make whatever contribution was needed at the time.

"*Gracias, Abuelita,*" I said softly to Doña Althea as she clumped away.
     She didn't look at me, but she heard me say it and she didn't deny that
she was my relative. Her small head crowned with its great white braid
nodded a little. No hugs or confessions of love. We were all a little stiff, I
understood that. Family constellations are fixed things. They don't change
just because you've learned the names of the stars. (328)

The reality of Codi's loneliness and isolation as a child is not denied,
but new facts change the picture by making it more complete. Codi was
not an outsider rejected by the community, but a semi-acknowledged
insider whose relationships to the community were denied by her father,
hidden by many relatives, and completely unknown to Codi. The deadly
combination of secrecy and ignorance made it difficult for family members
to acknowledge her, much as they tried. When Codi learned the truth
about her family, her new understanding of the past altered what she
remembered about her childhood. She was able to see new things, and
remember old things in a new way, once her vision was cleared. This is
remarkably similar to being shown the "secret" to a well-known visual
illusion: whereas before only an ornate vase is visible, once one's eyes
know how and where to look, the silhouette of a face emerges on either
side of the vase. Similarly, we see that the past, like our perception of the
vase, is not as fixed as we imagined. Codi's pain as a child is still there, but
it is newly comforted by the knowledge that she was not, as she imagined
(remembered), alone.
     While Doc Homer and Codi both struggle with time because of what
might broadly be referred to as "memory problems," Kingsolver's third
narrator reminds the reader that memory isn't the only thing that affects
our understanding of time. Indeed, storytelling itself often causes slippage
between the past and present. Hallie Noline, Codi's sister, is absent from
the primary action of the novel, but present throughout the story in the
memories of both Codi and her father. Hallie is also present through
lengthy quotations from the letters she writes to Codi from Nicaragua.
Every once in awhile, for a paragraph or a few pages at a time, we hear
Hallie's voice. Like the other narrative voices, Hallie's is "time-impaired,"
but not from disability nor memory problems. Rather, Hallie's voice consistently demonstrates the problems of linear time simply because it is a
voice in a letter. "Right this minute I'm sitting in the rain," she writes, but
Codi encounters that sentence several weeks after it was written (88).
Hallie's present is Codi's past, and even Hallie's future is Codi's past, since
Hallie's assurances that "I'll write from Nica next" (88) have already been
realized through letters that have already been written but not yet received.

Kingsolver makes this point about letter writing and time even more clearly through the letters that Codi refuses to read after knowing that her sister had been kidnapped:

> In the meantime, Hallie's letters still came to the Post Office box. I knew she had mailed them before she was kidnapped, but their appearance frightened me. They looked postmarked and cheerful and real, but they were ghosts, mocking what I'd believed was a solid connection between us. I'd staked my heart on that connection. If I could still get letters like this when Hallie was gone or in trouble, what had I ever really had?
>
> I didn't read them. I saved them. I would open them all once I'd heard her voice on the phone. I wouldn't be fooled again. (263)

Through the use of Hallie's letters, especially at the critical point of the novel when Hallie is missing, Kingsolver demonstrates to us that in the common experience of writing and receiving letters, the reality of time becomes more complex than our language's tense system can handle, and more complex than we normally recognize. This is most clear when Codi finally reads the letters that she saved to open all at once: she receives a letter that was written immediately following one that Codi had read weeks earlier. As Codi explains: "I'd forgotten that her last letter, which I'd read on the trip to Santa Rosalia, was a tirade . . . Two hours after she mailed that, she had written a pained apology that reached me now, a lifetime later. Any one moment can be like this, I thought. A continental divide" (298). The continental divide in time was not between the tirade and the apology, but between the reading of the first letter and the reading of the second; time *as measured by the letters* was moving in a profoundly different way for Hallie and for Codi.

The choice to use letters to tell a story, especially when only used for one of several narrators, forces us to reflect on both the time difficulties inherent in telling stories, and the even more pressing difficulties inherent in the attempt to understand the past as fixed and unitary. After all, the intrusion of a letter into a story usually provides information about the past, and that almost invariably alters the present. Even the simple act of receiving a letter is an acknowledgement that some part of the past has been, until now, unknown and unknowable to the letter's recipient. Hallie's letters add more than a new voice to Codi's narrated portions of the novel; they add a new complexity to Codi's experience of what is happening now, what has happened already, and what is going to happen, because none of these categories remains fixed once Hallie's letters intrude on Codi's supposedly linear life.

Choosing New Boundaries: The Day of the Dead

In addition to what we have discussed up to this point, Kingsolver uses a single overriding structure to shape the plot of her story. The event that forms and shapes the plot of *Animal Dreams* is the Day of the Dead, which Kingsolver uses to begin, center, and conclude the novel. The choice of this recurring celebration as an anchor for the story reveals three significant things. First, by choosing a repeating calendrical date to structure the time sequence of the novel, the hidden circularity of progressive time is revealed. Ancient peoples may have relied exclusively on cyclical time, but we haven't abandoned it completely. We can't, after all, as long as the recurrence of the seasons plays a large part in our experience of the world. Second, by choosing a holiday focused on death and the past, the fragile yet very real continuity of family life is emphasized. Finally, by locating key plot events in these structurally significant chapters, the importance of the *artificial* structure of the story is revealed. Each of these three elements will be considered in turn.

Marking Time in a Circle

The Day of the Dead happens every year. It is not a singular event, like a wedding, a birth, or a death: a story structured around a trio of weddings, births, or deaths may well emphasize the similarity or continuity between the events, but only in the clear context of their differences. In contrast, a yearly holiday like Christmas or the Day of the Dead manages to keep an overarching sameness through time. The details differ every year, but the essential *event* is the same. By choosing a recurring holiday, Kingsolver reminds us that we do in fact mark time in a circle, even as we insist on its linearity. The calendar returns to the same major events every year; we change and grow, but the calendar (time) remains the same.

This is not to say that we experience time as cyclical in a traditional religious sense, nor do Kingsolver's characters; they are modern people, and live in history, not in a world that is reborn every spring. But we discover that time-as-history-moving-forward is not annulled by the repetition of dates on the calendar; rather, it is given a fullness and depth impossible to conceive in a strictly linear (two-dimensional) understanding. Time here has three dimensions, not just two. History in *Animal Dreams* is not merely left behind like a road one has driven down on the way somewhere else; instead, history exists as both past and touchable present. The dead are dead, but they are still a part of life; the past is gone, but we are obligated to remember it. Kingsolver's characters are able to connect to the past and to people who were part of the past because of the recurrence of events, especially the Day of the Dead, that link the present with the past through ritual and repetition.

The three celebrations of the Day of the Dead that mark the beginning, center, and end of *Animal Dreams* are each identified differently in their titles given in the table of contents. Once again, Kingsolver's careful structuring is at issue here: the day is marked as the same, and yet different each time; it is experienced as new and yet as connected to what has come before. In the first chapter, "The Night of All Souls," Doc Homer watches his two girls sleep after a day at the cemetery. This night is an ending, a negating of the Day of the Dead/Day of All Souls, for this is when Doc Homer decides to cut his children off from this celebration in the future. The central chapter of the novel is titled simply "Day of the Dead," and it is here that Codi learns not only what this celebration is about, but is given a hint that she might, in fact, be a part of it (she discovered the grave of Homero Nolina, and began to suspect that he might be a relative of hers).

Finally, the concluding chapter of the novel is titled "Day of All Souls," and this title is a combination of the previous two. It echoes the title of the opening, and shifts the focus from night to day (or from death to new life). It also echoes the title of the central chapter, while shifting the focus there from the dead to their living souls. It is here that the reader learns of Codi's pregnancy, and it is here, too, that we see Codi both tending her father's grave and travelling with Viola to the place where she (Codi) saw her mother die. Unlike the opening chapter, in which the great-grandmothers are declared to be "no part of this family" (3), here at the novel's end Codi's great-grandmothers and other ancestors are lovingly tended, and linked to the new life Codi carries within her. She had longed to be part of "one of these living, celebrated families . . . with bones in the ground for roots" (165), and has discovered that she was always a part of one of them. Moreover, she has made the choice to celebrate that connection, to continue its life through her actions. As Codi moves forward into the future, the recurring event of the Day of the Dead will link her always to her past and her family's past. Time functions for her in both a linear and cyclical manner: it moves on, but remains connected to what has gone before.

Marking Time as a Family

The second way in which the Day of the Dead functions to structure the plot of the novel is through its focus on the life, death, and continuity of families. By choosing this particular device to structure the story, Kingsolver makes it clear to the reader that this is not merely Codi's story, even if the majority of it is told in her voice. Instead, this is a novel about a family—an entire family, some of whose members are dead, some alive, and some yet to be born. That the Day of the Dead shifts the reader's attention from the individual to the family is clear in each of the three chapters dealing with the holiday, but it is most obvious in the central chapter of the novel, when what has seemed to be Codi's story is revealed to be a much more complex tale. In this chapter of *Animal Dreams*, Codi attends the Day of the Dead celebration in Grace for the first time since she was a small child. As an outsider to this family ritual, she gains a perspective on it that helps many of us understand a holiday that is unfamiliar to the majority of Americans:

> Some graves had shrines with niches peopled by saints; some looked like botanical gardens of paper and silk; others had the initials of loved ones spelled out on the mound in white stones. The unifying principle was that the simplest thing was done with the greatest care. It was a comfort to see this attention lavished on the dead. In these families you would never stop being loved . . . Golden children ran wild over a field of dead great-grandmothers and great-grandfathers, and the bones must have wanted to rise up and knock together and rattle with joy. I have never seen a town that gave so much—so much of what *counts*—to its children.
>
> More than anything else I wished I belonged to one of these living, celebrated families, lush as plants, with bones in the ground for roots. I wanted pollen on my cheeks and one of those calcium ancestors to decorate as my own. Before we left at sunset I borrowed a marigold from Emelina's great-aunt Pocha, who wouldn't miss it. I ran back to lay it on Homero Nolina, just in case. (163, 165)

What Codi notices is, first, that the dead are part of their living families. The dead are not assumed to be gone, unreachable, located only in the past, but instead are part of a family's living and ongoing tradition. "In these families you would never stop being loved," Codi marvels, amazed. Significantly, Codi never visits her mother's grave, and indeed it seems as if it somehow might not exist (she does not find it nor even mention it during any of her trips to the cemetery). Doc Homer never speaks of his wife to either Codi or Hallie; in the Noline family, unlike every family in Grace, the dead are erased from existence. Secondly, she realizes that this is a holiday about the past and the dead that is celebrated most enthusiastically by the children; indeed, the entire event seems in some ways to be *for* the children. "I have never seen a town that gave so much—so much of what counts—to its children," Codi remarks, having seen that a day in which the dead are fed and graves are tended is a day not only to honor those who are gone but to introduce the dead to those among the living who have never known them. The children playing in the graveyard know that they are part of a beloved family "with bones in the ground for roots," and while they presumably are focused almost exclusively on the candy and the cookies and the play, the overall experience is much different than Halloween, whose focus on candy and ghosts is superficially similar. The experience of the Day of the Dead, in contrast to the experience of Halloween, is an experience of family. It is also an experience of the reality of the dead, not of imaginary ghosts and goblins. For children who celebrate both in quick succession (the Day of the Dead, November 2, comes two days after Halloween, October 31), the two holidays are certainly linked, but it is clear even to the young which day is "just for fun" and which brims with unspoken importance.

Marking Time to Organize the Story

Thus the plot device of the Day of the Dead provides the reader with both an understanding of the family nature of *Animal Dreams* and an understanding of the novel's different approach to time as a combination of linear and circular. Finally, Kingsolver's use of the Day of the Dead as a structuring device also emphasizes the constructed nature of her tale, and indeed of all tales: it is impossible to tell a story without "grasping together" many separate events into an account of an action with a beginning, middle, and end. By insisting that the Day of the Dead open and conclude the novel, instead of just serving as the centerpiece, Kingsolver reminds the reader that emplotment is a process of human choice and human creation. Moreover, it is this human choice and creation that tame the chaos of time, that, in effect, redeem time itself. Kingsolver's entire novel works toward this goal of redeeming time: certainly the construction of its plot must contribute, too, to the reader's growing sense that time is not the relentless, unconquerable outside force we have always considered it to be. By including the opening chapter, set twenty years before the main part of the tale, and the concluding chapter, set several years after, Kingsolver reminds the reader that no slice of time is complete without its past and its future. Codi's story, as told from chapters two through twenty-seven, would work fairly well as the story of a young woman's redemptive return home; but it would be incomplete, having left out of its structure one of its most important themes, that of time and the interconnection between the separate "places" we normally designate as past, present, and future. By constructing *Animal Dreams* as a story of time, Kingsolver demonstrates that the stories we tell can conquer time; by emphasizing the artificially constructed nature of her tale, she reminds the reader that it is our choice to embrace this creative, constructive act, or be overwhelmed by time's destructive power. Time is indeed open, redemption is indeed possible, and we know both of these things only through narrative, which exists through the act of emplotment, by which our world comes into being.

Shifting Sands, Changing Times

Kingsolver, of course, did not limit herself to careful attention only to the structure and narration of the novel. While these have immense power to shape a reader's experience, there are other, sometimes surprising, ways to draw our attention toward time and how it works. The *setting* of *Animal Dreams* turns out to be a key element in Kingsolver's effort to reconstruct our understanding of time. The idea that place can affect our understanding of time may seem unusual; after all, time passes no matter where we may find ourselves. However, since we are looking at our *experience* of time, it is important to remember that no aspect of our experience can be completely isolated from the all the others. Where we are, then, will affect how we experience the passage of time. This can happen in several ways. One is that a particular place can be experienced as exciting or boring. For example, an elementary school student may see a classroom as a place where time all but stops and a playground as a place where time always goes by far too quickly. Another way that place can influence time is that a structure or landscape may be the site of a memory, either personal or historical. Personal examples might include the house one grew up in; cultural examples could include Gettysburg or any other historical landmark. Standing "right where it all happened" can sometimes bring the past very close; on the other hand, given the changes that often occur over time, it can make the past seem very distant indeed. Finally, we have preconceived notions about how time passes in certain types of places. For example, the stereotype would indicate that time moves more quickly in the busy city than in the quiet countryside. Isolated small towns are said to be "stuck in the past," and stories taking place in settings such as the moon and Mars clearly indicate (without bothering to mention it explicitly) a future time. All of these elements come into play for us as we read *Animal Dreams*, for the setting is an inextricable part of the our experience of the passage of time.

Codi's home, Grace, Arizona, is a small town in rural, desert Arizona, built into a canyon whose river sustains the life of the community and its orchards. Both the rural aspect of the setting and the desert will prove to be significant. Grace is also a "company town," built near a mine that not only assaulted the earth around Grace but also poisoned its water. The mere idea of a company town places the story within a particular historical context, and the emphasis on the environmental consequences of that existence enables the reader to measure the passage of time by noticing the relative health or decline of the land. In addition, the Anglo town of Grace, with its particular relationship between the human inhabitants and the land, is contrasted strikingly with two Native American settlements nearby, one still inhabited and one abandoned in an unknown, prehistoric past.

The desert setting that Kingsolver chose for *Animal Dreams* is significant in several ways. First, the landscape of a desert seems to the human eye to change very little over time: rocks and sand tend to look the same no matter what the season, unlike the trees and crops of more temperate climes. This illusion of timelessness, combined with the awe often inspired by beautiful but terrifyingly inhuman wilderness, gives rise to thoughts of eternity. To contrast this, Kingsolver brings out a second significant aspect of this particular desert: it is dying, being murdered by its human inhabitants. The combination of hints of eternity alongside intimations of apocalypse unsettles the reader, who is unsure about whether the place inhabited by Kingsolver's characters is timeless and still or rushing headlong towards destruction. Third, the choice of a desert setting in a conversion story has clearly Christian overtones, bringing to mind the desert fathers and a long Christian tradition of finding God in the fierce wilderness. Codi's story and its comfortably contemporary setting is thus joined forcefully to ancient stories and faraway places; it is the desert that makes this connection. Finally, Kingsolver's desert is home to the dead more than to the living: the graveyards are by far the most important aspect of each human habitation she describes. This focus on the dead in the midst of a story of the living works to call the reader's attention persistently away from the present and into the past. Each of these aspects of the setting of *Animal Dreams*—the desert as image of eternity, site of the apocalypse, memory of Christian history, and home of the dead—will be discussed in turn.

Image of Eternity

One way to attempt to describe eternity is the absence of time. This stillness, or timelessness, is rarely evident in a landscape of our ever-growing, ever-moving, ever-changing earth—except in a desert. The timelessness of a desert setting would seem to apply more to the wilderness of the desert, but Kingsolver points out that even human constructions such as houses and even entire towns take on the stopped-in-time quality more obvious in bare rocks surrounded by a sea of featureless sand. When Codi first arrives in Grace, she is unsettled by how much she does not remember nor recognize in a place that must still be the same as when she left:

It was midmorning when I stepped down off the bus in Grace, and I didn't recognize it. Even in fourteen years it couldn't have changed much, though, so I knew it was just me. Grace is made of things that erode too slowly to be noticed: red granite canyon walls, orchards of sturdy old fruit trees past their prime, a shamelessly unpolluted sky. The houses were built in no big hurry back when labor was taken for granted, and now were in no big hurry to decay. Arthritic mesquite trees grew out of impossible crevices in the cliffs, looking as if they could adapt to life on Mars if need be. (8)

The "things that erode too slowly to be noticed" are primarily natural: rocks, trees, and sky. However, the homes of Grace, built carefully and solidly long ago, possess a character that enable them to nest neatly between Codi's description of "unpolluted sky" and "arthritic mesquite trees." Like the natural aspects of the desert, the human artifacts as well seem caught in a stasis, unaffected by time.

If this is true of Grace, it is even more true of the Native American pueblos that Codi visited with Loyd. The prehistoric pueblo at Kinishba, abandoned by its inhabitants some eight hundred years ago, still stands gracefully "out there in the middle of God's backyard . . . made entirely of carefully set stone, no mortar" (127). Unlike Grace, which seemed completely unfamiliar to Codi, the pueblo struck her as "something familiar" (129). Her sense of recognition came not from ever having seen the pueblo before, but from her training in biology:

I couldn't stop running my eyes over the walls and the low, even roofline. The stones were mostly the same shape, rectangular, but all different sizes; there would be a row of large stones, and then two or three thinner rows, then a couple of middle-sized rows. There was something familiar about the way they fit together. In a minute it came to me. They looked just like cells under a microscope.

"It doesn't even look like it was built," I said. "It's too beautiful. It looks like something alive that just *grew* here." (129; emphasis in original)

Codi's sense of the building's organic, living quality is paradoxical in the face of its long abandonment. The paradox deepens when Loyd points out to her that "the walls are graveyards," filled with the bones of dead family members, mortared into the walls so as to remain close to loved ones, even in death (128). The pueblo is a human construction that looks natural, an ancient construction that has not decayed, and it is built out of the dead but appears to be a living organism. These contrasts and dissonances serve to make the pueblo yet another way that the novel attacks the reader's assumptions, and again, at the heart of the paradoxes is the problem of time—or rather, several faces of this complex problem. Is time, like the pueblo, a human construction or does it exist naturally? If we recognize the passage of time by growth and decay, how do we recognize it in something that does neither? And if one definitive way to mark out the difference between the past and the present is the difference between the dead and the living, how can something dead contribute to new life? This last is clearly not only a problem of time but of the Christian story itself. The pairing of death and new life is central not only in the story of Jesus' passion and resurrection, but in the traditional story we tell of how our own lives move from sin to salvation, from death to new life.

The mere existence of this prehistoric structure brings the problem of time to mind, and shifts the reality of the past firmly into the present. Further emphasizing both issues, Codi reflects on the pueblo and its former inhabitants in a way that links the dead and the living. She tries to imagine what it would have been like to live in the pueblo in its prime, when it was not silent and still but full of life, noise, and activity. She envisions "stepping from room to room over sleeping couples, listening through all the noises of cooking and scolding and washing up for the sound of your own kids, who would know secret shortcuts to their friends' apartments" (128). In Codi's mind, the former inhabitants of the pueblo are not strange ancient beings, barely human and unfathomable, but instead people just like her, whose concerns would fit in remarkably well in her time and her hometown. The noise of "cooking and scolding and washing up" is, in her understanding, eternal, as is the propensity of children to have secrets and best friends and the desire to avoid their parents when there is work to be done. Certainly the lives of the Pueblo Indians almost a thousand years ago were staggeringly different than Codi's life in Grace, and even Loyd's life in the Santa Rosalia Pueblo, but Kingsolver has Codi make the connection between the two, and draw the past and its people into the present, if only for a moment.

The timelessness of desert pueblos is emphasized not only in Codi and Loyd's visit to the abandoned Kinishba pueblo, but also in their visit to Santa Rosalia Pueblo, Loyd's family home. It is during this few days that Codi realizes that Loyd is not "a TV Indian . . . dumb but cute" (181), nor a "museum piece," someone who can be identified merely by those historical aspects of his culture now housed in glass boxes for tourists to examine.[7] Instead, Loyd is very much a contemporary of hers—one with a far different community, history, and family, but a contemporary all the same. His home is a pueblo just like Kinishba but a pueblo whose residents inhabit the twentieth century quite comfortably:

It was a village of weathered rectangles, some stacked stepwise in twos
and threes, the houses all blending into one another around a central
plaza. The stone walls were covered with adobe plaster, smooth and
appealing as mud pies: a beautiful brown town . . . One house had a basketball hoop nailed to the end beams. . . Loyd's mother's house had a
green door. The front window was crowded with artificial flowers and
ceramic animals. (227)

Like Kinishba, the Santa Rosalia Pueblo was built like living cells nes-
tled in the earth: stacked, rectangular buildings in infinite shades of brown,
"built on a mesa and blended perfectly with the landscape, constructed of
the same stones as the outcroppings that topped all the other, empty
mesas" (227). But Kinishba was ancient and abandoned, a historical relic
that only emphasized that "Indians are . . . people that lived a long time
ago."[8] Santa Rosalia, on the other hand, was full of life—life that effortlessly combined ancient Pueblo traditions with the trappings of modern
American society. Again, the past is brought into the present, and the persistence and continuity of Native American society is emphasized. Even
though Pueblo life has obviously changed in eight hundred years, its basic
contours and values, as expressed in building, beauty, and dance, have
remained stable. Despite the addition of basketball and artificial flowers,
Pueblo culture retains an aspect of timelessness that Kingsolver points to
in her carefully constructed descriptions of the similarities between
Kinishba and Santa Rosalia.

Site of Apocalypse

To contrast with the timelessness of the desert and its isolated places of
human habitation, Kingsolver focuses on the fragility and impending
destruction of much of the seemingly eternal places she describes. The environmental ravaging of the earth has brought the raging destruction of the
apocalypse into the restful stillness of desert places. The Black Mountain
Mining Company is poisoning Grace's river with sulfuric acid run through
the mine tailings, while another mining company destroys mountains
nearby in search of a kind of rock called pumice, which "was required for
the manufacture of so-called distressed denim jeans" (240). Even the fields
around Grace that grew alfalfa as recently as Codi's childhood were
"abandoned now, like half the cropland in Arizona, salted to death by
years of bad irrigation . . . the white soil gleam[ed] like a boneyard" (50).

As Codi gradually comes to think of Grace as home, the ecological
destruction of the town, its river, its orchards, and the desert surrounding

all these things moves from being an interesting rumor to an overriding obsession for her. "Poison ground" is no longer a strange phrase overheard at a party, half-understood and wholly unconnected to Codi's life. Instead, it is a clear and frightening account of the earth around her. As she and her biology class discovered:

> Our water was dead. It might as well have come from a river on the moon . . . The pH, which we tested, from some areas came in just a hair higher than battery acid . . . [I] filed an affidavit with local authorities on the pH and biotic death of the river.

The images of ecological destruction become more and more vivid as Codi learns about what is happening to the land near her home. Orchards covered with fallen immature fruit, or "fruit drop" (56), are not nearly as threatening as a river devoid of microscopic life, but both are the result of sulfuric acid being dumped in the river. Later, the new dam under construction at the mine, which will divert the river out of Grace and effectively kill the town, is described as "look[ing] exactly like what it was—a huge grave" (161). Finally, Codi's nearly hysterical lecture to her biology class on pollution and environmental destruction around the world is given shape and its ultimate impact through her comparison of the ozone layer to the face shields worn by workers in the mine smelter:

> "People can forget, and forget, and forget, but the land has a memory. The lakes and the rivers are still hanging on to the DDT and every other insult we ever gave them. Lake Superior is a superior cesspool. The fish have cancer. The ocean is getting used up. The damn *air* is getting used up." I pointed at the ceiling, meaning to indicate the sky. "You know what's up there? Ozone" . . . I surveyed the class thoughtfully and demanded, "Whose Dad or Mom ever worked in the smelter?"
>
> About half the hands went up, reluctantly.
>
> "You know what they did up there, right? One way or another they were around thousand-degree hot metal. You ever see them dressed for work? They wore coveralls like Mr. Neil Armstrong walking on the moon, and a big shield over their faces . . . Imagine that's you, working up there with that hot metal in your face. Now, somebody rips that mask off you while you're working. Goodbye face. Goodbye nose and eyelids, beauty queens. You're dead . . . That's what the ozone layer does for us, boys and girls, it's a big face shield in the sky . . . And it's slipping away from us. There's a big hole in it over the South Pole."(255–56)

The rhetoric Codi uses is part of a new narrative of world destruction that has been called "ecological apocalyptic." Unlike traditional, religious apocalyptic narratives, which promise a renewal of the world after its violent destruction, ecological apocalyptic offers no such hope. Rather, its message is one of the imminent possibility of permanent, global destruction of the earth and all its inhabitants. This terrifying apocalyptic scenario contrasts strongly with the peaceful images of the timeless pueblos and stunning, seemingly unchanging rock formations of the desert. We end up feeling tossed mercilessly between images of eternity and of the apocalyptic end of time, and each alters our understanding of the other. Suddenly the eternal looks fragile and finite, while apocalyptic endings seem unimaginable in the face of the beauty and history they would destroy forever. Neither forever nor the end of all is as easily imagined as it once was. The desert setting of the story has reminded us of how difficult it is to grasp either time's finite nature or its infinite expanse, especially as we do not know which is the "real" nature of time.

Memory of Christian History

Besides these great questions of eternity and apocalypse, Kingsolver's desert setting also brings to mind a smaller issue of time, that of the association of the history of Christianity with the desert. This association, of course, begins in the time of the Hebrew Scriptures, in which "the God of Sinai . . . thrives on fierce landscapes, seemingly forcing God's people into wild and wretched climes where trust must be absolute."[9] Jesus, like his ancestors, is "'driven' into the desert . . . forced to take the hard way, going directly from his baptism into the wilderness of temptation . . . headed already toward the cross."[10] In every century since, Christian monastics and other spiritual seekers followed, and have constructed a spiritual understanding of desert places and desert encounters with God that links the wilderness inextricably with the divine.

Codi, in her journey of conversion set in the Arizona desert, is thus joined with all the pilgrims who have traversed this desert way before her. As with Kingsolver's insistence through her use of the Day of the Dead that *Animal Dreams* is not merely Codi's story but is a story of a family, it is also clear through Kingsolver's use of the desert as a setting that Codi's story is not located merely in 1985, but is joined in a powerful way to stories that took place in times as far removed as the second-century Egyptian desert, home to St. Anthony and the other Desert Fathers of the early church. The differences in people's lives over that great stretch of time is connected through a similarity of place (a desert), and it is that desert and its recurrence in spiritual history that enable Codi's story to share in the weight and meaning of more history than she knows or can even imagine.

Home of the Dead

Finally, Kingsolver's desert setting focuses the reader's attention on time because the desert is the home of the dead, not the living. One of the most prominent features of Kinishba is its thick walls, containing the bones of the dead; one of the most significant events in Codi's visit to the Santa Rosalia pueblo was her discovery of a picture of Leander, Loyd's dead twin. Grace's center of gravity is its cemetery, where the history of Grace's families lives on in the lovingly tended graves. The desert itself is often feared as a place where death is an uncomfortably real possibility: between the lack of water, long stretches of uninhabited land, sparseness of edible food, and extremes of cold and heat, the desert is not kind to unprepared wanderers. In setting the life of her story and characters in the midst of death, and in the midst of the memory of the dead, Kingsolver reminds us yet again that, as Faulkner so wonderfully put it, "The past is never dead. It's not even past."[11]

Dangerous Memories, Living Hope

Constructing a story involves more than just the "building blocks" of setting, narration, and structure that we've discussed so far. The *themes* of a novel often reflect or reinforce ideas that we begin to see in the structure or setting. Thus, our final task is to explore the themes of *Animal Dreams* with respect to both time and women. We have seen, so far, that time can be experienced as open and that redemption of the past is possible, but what does that mean for the experience of women in the novel? Two of Kingsolver's themes are at issue here, and both have as much to do with women as they do with time and redemption.

First, one of the themes of *Animal Dreams* is that we are not alone, especially during an experience of conversion, or serious change in our lives. The community in which we live is part of who we are, and is a necessary part of any change that happens to us. From a theological standpoint, Codi's conversion to a new life, impossible without the presence of many others, both dead and living, might be read as a statement about how the communion of saints functions as a redemptive force in the world. What a marvelous thought! The invisible presence of our beloved dead can work in positive ways in the world. This is not to say that "ghosts" work miracles around us, but that the community of those who love God is wider than we sometimes imagine. In more formal terms, we can explain the power of the communion of saints through the concept of "dangerous memory," which affects our understanding of how history, and thus time, actually works. Both dangerous memory and the communion of saints will be discussed further below.

The second prominent theme relating to time redefines the nature of hope. The hope that Hallie displays in her commitment to a new life in Nicaragua is a different kind of hope than we might expect, for it is a hope that is lived out in the present rather than focused exclusively on the future. Moreover, Kingsolver demonstrates that Codi's distinct lack of hope is rooted not just in her unhappy past, but in her belief that the past is fixed and unchangeable. Surprising things are happening here; clearly, we need to look closely at how hope functions in the novel, and how it is related to the present and past as well as to the future.

First, though, we turn to the communion of saints. Before we can judge whether or not the community Codi encountered in Grace could be considered a communion of saints, we need some theological background. Catholic theologian Elizabeth Johnson reminds us that the communion of saints does not, as many might assume, refer primarily to those special people the tradition has set apart as "saints." Instead, the idea of the communion of saints refers to *the whole Christian community*, including both the dead and the living. It even stretches beyond the human, embracing all of God's creatures and all of creation, in "the cosmic community of life, which is also sacred. Ultimately it points to the Creator Spirit who . . . makes holy the world."[12]

This is a fascinating and lovely description of the communion of saints. It embraces the dead as well as the living, animals as well as human beings, and acknowledges that we often find reminders of the sacred in God's creation around us. Consider, after all, Codi and the things, people, and events that pushed her along the path of conversion. The agents of change that Codi encountered in Grace consist primarily of her friends, neighbors, students, and relatives, but also include Spider Rock, the pueblo at Kinishba, the graveyard (and its inhabitants) in Grace, and even Loyd's dog, Jack. This community makes Codi's conversion and redemption possible: the changes that happen in her life are not due to choices made in isolation, but rather to the dawn of a relationship "flowing among an intergenerational company of persons profoundly touched by the sacred, sharing in the cosmic community of life which is also sacred."[13] Because of the new and redemptive relationships that have reshaped her life, Codi becomes part of Grace, and not only chooses to live there and tend the family graves, but to continue her family through becoming pregnant. Her new life in Grace is symbolized by the rebirth of the dead land surrounding the town:

> We reached the crest of the canyon where the white salt crust of the old alfalfa fields began. Dead for two decades, the earth was long and white and cracked, like a huge porcelain platter dropped from the heavens. But now the rabbitbrush was beginning to grow here too, topped with brushy gold flowers, growing like a renegade crop in the long, straight troughs of the old irrigation ditches. (341)

Thus in the final chapter of *Animal Dreams*, we see Codi connected not only to her dead ancestors and future child, but to a renewal of the earth. The redeeming experiences she has undergone shine forth in her body (the pregnancy), her actions (tending Doc Homer's grave), and the earth around her. The communion of saints is truly with her in all its splendor, as she begins her new life in Grace in a new kind of time that incorporates the past, present, and future in a complex dance of love, memory, and hope.

This redeeming combination of love, memory, and hope is described theologically through the idea of "dangerous memory," which is a "kind of remembering [that] challenges the absolute power of the present and brings to mind a future that is still outstanding."[14] That future is defined as the Kingdom of God, in which the dignity and freedom of God's people will at last be honored. As Sharon Welch explains:

> Dangerous memories fund a community's sense of dignity; they inspire and empower those who challenge oppression. Dangerous memories are a people's history of resistance and struggle, of dignity and transcendence in the face of oppression.
>
> Dangerous memories are stories of defeat and of victory, a casting of the past in terms of a present of joy, hope, and struggle.[15]

For Christians, dangerous memories include everything from the Exodus to Roman persecution of early Christian communities to stories of present-day mission workers. And, of course, the dangerous memory at the heart of Christian faith is our memory of the death and resurrection of Jesus. In *Animal Dreams*, there are at least two dangerous memories that come to prominence: the first is the memory of the Gracela sisters, and the second is the memory of Hallie. Both energize their communities, empowering those who are left behind. Both are tales of joy, hope, and struggle that live on long after the protagonist's death.

In the case of the Gracela sisters, it was the legend of their journey to Grace that gave the inhabitants of the town the strength and dignity to fight for the survival of Grace's river and orchards. The importance of the sisters is made clear not only in Codi's fascination with their story and in Doc Homer's efforts to document the genetic anomaly present in their descendents, but most significantly during the television interview in which the plans of the Black Mountain Mining Company are exposed to the world. Doña Althea is being interviewed about the peacock piñatas that had become "a hot decorator item in gentrified adobe neighborhoods like the one in Tucson that Hallie used to call Barrio Volvo" (263), and ends up telling the story of the Gracelas, who brought the first peacocks to Grace:

> Doña Althea lifted her head, adjusted her shawl, leaned back and put her hands on her knees, which were spread wide apart under her black skirt. "*Hace cien años*," she began. "More than one hundred years ago, my mother and her eight sisters came to this valley from Spain to bring light and happiness to the poor miners, who had no wives. They were the nine Gracela sisters: Althea, Renata, Hilaria, Carina, Julietta, Ursolina, Violetta, Camila, and Estrella."
>
> She pronounced the names musically and slowly, drawing out the syllables and rolling the r's. They were the names of fairy princesses, but the story, in her high, sustained voice, was Biblical. It was the Genesis of Grace. And of Hallie and me. Our father's own grandmother—mother of Homero Nolina up in the graveyard—was one of those princesses: the red-haired, feisty one. I could picture her barefoot, her hair curly like Hallie's and coming loose from its knot. I saw her standing in the open front door of her house, shaking a soup spoon at her sisters' arrogant children who came to tease her own. Perhaps she was Ursolina, the little bear . . . I don't know what they heard on the CBS news. I heard a bedtime story thirty years late. (267–68)

The story that Doña Althea told not only served as a source of identity and dignity in Codi's life that she recognized as biblical in importance, but was also clearly that important for most of the inhabitants of Grace, who knew the story far better than did Codi. By telling this story and creating the peacock piñatas that prompted the interview, Doña Althea set into motion the activity that would, in the end, save the town: it was through his interest in the piñatas and the historical town from which they came that Sean Rideheart came to Grace and told the women how to initiate the process of designating their town and their orchards as a National Historic Preserve.

The memory of the Gracela sisters gave Grace its name and identity, and it also identified the town as founded by women. Here we see glimpses of the idea that women are historical actors; women, too, are protagonists of history. The phrase "protagonist of history" comes from a letter that Hallie wrote to Codi, in which she quoted one of the priests she worked with: "Father Fernando Cardenal, who was in charge of the literacy crusade [said]: 'You learn to read so you can identify the reality in which you live, so that you can become a protagonist of history rather than a spectator'" (326). If you recall that the Western shift to historical, linear time led to a distorted view of women as the source of limitation and death, then you realize that understanding women as protagonists of history—the good guys!—is new, and important. When women are not only sources of death but *symbols* of death, it is hard to see women as individual historical actors in their own right. Yet here in Grace, the Gracela sisters are not emblems of decay or mortality, even though their bones lie in the graveyard. Rather, they are the revered founders of a town and a family that is fighting for its survival. Moreover, the town and the family depend on their heritage—on the memory of these women—to know how to fight. Why don't they fight like "normal" activists, writing letters, protesting, marching, perhaps resorting to sabotage? "We don't write such good letters," Doña Althea tells the interviewer when he asks why they don't simply write to their congressman. She continues:

> I don't think we have any congressman out here anyway, do we? . . . And also we don't know how to use dynamite. What we know how to do is make nice things out of paper. Flowers, piñatas, *cascarones*. And we sew things. That's what we ladies here do. (266–67)

Doña Althea is, of course, being modest in a very sly way. She knows exactly what she and her friends have done, even as she downplays its significance for the TV interview. What the ladies of Grace do is save their town when no one else can; what they do is rely on their memory and their heritage to find a way toward a future. The dangerous memory of the Gracela sisters identifies women as *agents of change* and even as *saviors* (bringing "light and happiness to the poor miners" [267]). Having been raised with the heritage of these dangerous memories, the women of Grace in the 1980s are able to see themselves as capable of taking on "The Mountain" and saving their town.

While the memory of the nine Gracela sisters is treasured by the entire town of Grace, and has been elevated over time to the status of legend, the dangerous memory of Hallie's life is still young, but embraced by people from places as far-flung as Minnesota and Nicaragua. Hallie's life, short though it had been, was full of the kind of energy that would continue to touch people long after her death. As Loyd told Codi, "A life like your sister's isn't some little pony you can turn around any way you want. It's a train. Once it gets going it's heavier than heaven and hell put together and it runs on its own track" (304). Hallie's track led her to Nicaragua, and to a life Codi could barely imagine:

> I'd gotten a card from a nun in Minneapolis who had known Hallie . . . She met Hallie at the clinic in Chinandega the day Hallie brought in a child who'd drunk paraquat from a Coke bottle. Sister Martin and Hallie sat with the child the whole day, and she said that although I might not think it possible, she felt she'd come to know Hallie well during that time . . .
>
> She said thousands of people joined us in mourning Hallie. "I know that doesn't make your grief any smaller," she wrote. "But I believe it makes Hallie's presence larger. Certainly, she won't be forgotten." (314, 326)

Like most of the anonymous saints in the community of saints, Hallie will in fact someday be forgotten. Certainly it needs to be remembered here that Hallie is a fictional character, and not a "real" member of the community of saints. However, Hallie's life, work, death, and impact on others can be compared to that of Ben Linder, to whom the novel is dedicated. Linder was, like Hallie, a volunteer worker in Nicaragua who was murdered by the contras; unlike Hallie, he was entirely real. Linder "was a hydroelectric engineer in his twenties from Portland, Oregon . . . whose family I dearly love and whose death is permanently grieved."[16] Linder, like Hallie, touched people by his life and his death. His memory inspired others; indeed, it inspired Barbara Kingsolver to write *Animal Dreams*. Similarly, within the world imagined by the novel, Hallie's existence and her memory inspired others. The dangerous memory of Hallie's life had its greatest impact on her sister, Codi. "Everything we'd been I was now," Codi reflected at Hallie's memorial service, thus taking on the burden and the dream of living not just for herself but for her sister and the things and people Hallie loved (328). And in adopting this new, wider life, Codi is able to stay in Grace, and to tell her father about her own choices toward being a protagonist of history:

> "Did you know I'm a good science teacher? The kids and the teachers all voted. They say I'm spirited. How do you like that?"
>
> "It's what I would expect."
>
> "I'm teaching them how to have a cultural memory . . . I want them to be custodians of the earth." (332)

Thus, Codi is taking on as her life's work the passing on of dangerous memories, and the embrace of the community of saints who lived those memories. She, too, becomes a protagonist of history in her efforts to ensure that the next generation knows the stories and has a foundation from which to understand themselves and continue the struggle.

The second theme of *Animal Dreams* that relates to Kingsolver's project of refiguring time is that of hope, and it is intimately connected to the first. The communion of saints exists in hope, and it is a hope that is in every way unlike the everyday meaning of the word. In commonplace terms, to hope is "to entertain a wish for something with some expectation," but the hope of the communion of saints is not based on a wish, nor is their commitment to hope as fragile as the word "entertain" implies. Instead, the hope sustained by the communion of saints is

> not necessarily aimed at anything specific but consists in "general confidence in God's protection and help." . . . In times of peace and blessing, hope gives thanks and expects further good. In times of affliction and distress hope, still directed toward God, longs for deliverance . . . For Israel, the ground of this hope lies in the Exodus narrative of passing over from slavery to freedom and a covenanted life . . . For the Christian community, the bedrock of hope, similarly directed toward God, became the paschal narrative of the death and resurrection of Jesus Christ. Here, too, hope oscillates between the arrival of the good in this world and expectation of a future for the living, the dead, and the whole cosmos in the glory of God.[17]

This hope, grounded in the memory of God's great deeds of power in the past—the Exodus, for example, and the resurrection of Jesus—affirms that God's very character teaches us that suffering is not the truth of our lives. More than that, we also know that death is not the end for us, because we know that God is faithful.[18] Moreover, this hope has a "creative function" in our lives here and now: as Johnson argues, the hope of the communion of saints does not lead us to avoid responsibility for this world, but instead "inspires people to put the imprint of hope on personal relationships, social structures, and ecological communities."[19] The transformative power of hope, then, affects every corner of life:

> Thus does transcendent hope work critically in the service of social justice. The final, God-given, blessed future provides a point of reference to which present injustices stand in sharp contrast and can be named for the abominations they truly are . . . Rather than be immobilized by the dead weight

of suffering, or by apathetic indifference before the pain of others, or by discouragement over the long haul yet to be made, those who live with transcendent hope drink from an unquenchable source of power, the promise of God that *nevertheless* something else will be possible.[20]

Hallie is motivated by this sort of hope as she travels to Nicaragua to work in the cotton fields, and discovers in her life there what it means to have hope as the driving force of her life, even when the main task of her life is to spend "one more morning in a muggy cotton field, checking the undersides of leaves to see what's been there, figuring out what to do that won't clear a path for worse problems next week" (299). The problems and work of her daily life are the measure of her hope; as she tells Codi:

> Wars and elections are both too big and too small to matter in the long run. The daily work—that goes on, it adds up. It goes into the ground, into crops, into children's bellies and their bright eyes. Good things don't get lost. (299)

This is a description of hope that is rooted in both the present and the future; it is not merely entertaining the idea of a possible forthcoming goodness, but is instead activity that works toward a blessed future, confident that the "fragments of well-being becom[ing] embodied in the world [are] real if transitory anticipations of the coming well-being, even here, even now."[21] Moreover, it is significant that the person in the novel who embodies the living hope of the communion of saints is a woman: she has not been destroyed nor erased by the limitations of historical, linear time. Instead, Hallie lives in a time that is shaped by the combination of her commitment to those she loves in the present, those who have inspired her in the past, and those who will someday live in the world she is helping to form. Hallie attempts to explain to Codi her understanding of hope and her commitment to life as shaped by that hope, but this is something that Codi does not and cannot grasp until after Hallie's death:

> Codi, here's what I've decided: the very least you can do in your life is to figure out what you hope for. And the most you can do is live inside that hope. Not admire it from a distance but live right in it, under its roof. What I want is so simple I almost can't say it: elementary kindness. Enough to eat, enough to go around. The possibility that kids might one day grow up to be neither the destroyers nor the destroyed. That's about it. Right now I'm living in that hope, running down its hallway and touching the walls on both sides.
> I can't tell you how good it feels. I wish you knew. (299)

Where Hallie embraces the notion of living in hope, and is able to live in the present because she is sustained by both the future and the "transitory anticipations" of that future that exist in her daily life, Codi (throughout most of *Animal Dreams*) instead rejects hope and lives in a present that has been completely and finally determined by the past. The past that haunts Codi is not the energizing past of dangerous memories, but rather the deadening past of loss, regret, and failure. Until she learns that her past was in fact wider than the few memories she retains of the death of her mother and the loss of the baby she miscarried as a teenager, she is unable to embrace the possibilities inherent in either the present or the future. Once Codi's past is transformed—once it includes the truth about her family and her connection to the community—her present is reborn as well. Instead of a present and future dedicated solely to fleeing the pain of the past, Codi is able to embrace a present and future that incorporate the truth of the past, and the dangerous memories that can aid her continuing struggle to live in hope. "I'm trying to figure out what I hope for," Codi tells her father as she buries the mementos of Hallie collected at her memorial service (333). "It's a most dangerous thing, hope," Doc Homer warns her in response, adding, "Hope involves giving a great deal of yourself away" (333). Yet as Codi has discovered, it also involves finding herself at last, and finding the truth of her life as part of a community of hope, and struggle, and love.

—m—

Codi's journey of conversion and redemption is a modern and rather secular tale, or at least it appears so on the surface. In its assumptions, however, and in its underlying commitments, it is a very old story of the power of Christian community and hope to transform a broken life into one that is not only beginning to heal but is capable of working toward the healing and wholeness of others. The most important thing about this particular conversion tale, however, is that it is constructed in such a way that the problem of time and redemption is highlighted throughout, and is addressed in a way that transforms not only Codi but those of us who read her story. Once we encounter not only Kingsolver's story but its structure, narration, setting, and themes, it becomes not only possible but necessary to conclude that time is not closed, but open; redemption is not a foolish dream, but a real possibility; and historical time, despite its misogynistic construction, has room for women as protagonists of history and of their own lives. Time itself has been refigured by the stylistic and narrative choices made by Kingsolver's emplotment of the events of Codi and

Hallie's lives. We are left with the joyful conclusion that time itself must be redeemable in the story God is telling all around us—in God's emplotment of the events of creation.

Notes

1. Barbara Kingsolver, *Animal Dreams* (New York: HarperCollins, 1990). Excerpts from *Animal Dreams* are copyright © 1990 by Barbara Kingsolver. Reprinted by permission of HarperCollins Publishers Inc. and Frances Goldin Literary Agency, Inc.

2. Marjorie Hewitt Suchocki, *God, Christ, Church: A Practical Guide to Process Theology*, rev. ed. (New York: Crossroad, 1989), 74–75.

3. Augustine, *Confessions* XI:14 (New York: Penguin, 1961), 264.

4. Paul Ricoeur, *Time and Narrative*, vol. 1, trans. Kathleen McLaughlin and David Pellauer (Chicago: University of Chicago Press, 1984), xi.

5. Ibid., x.

6. Ibid., 3.

7. Barbara Kingsolver, "The Spaces Between," in *High Tide in Tucson: Essays from Now or Never* (New York: HarperCollins, 1995), 157. When Codi is finally confronted with the reality of Loyd's family and home, her opinion about him undergoes a radical shift; she is able to begin to see him truly for the first time, and to strip away the dark lens of the stereotypes through which she had unwittingly constructed him as a mythical figure instead of a human being. This shift is something that Kingsolver wants her reader to undergo, too, since otherwise it would be too easy to romanticize Loyd as a "noble savage," especially given his role in Codi's conversion experiences.

8. Kingsolver, *High Tide in Tucson*, 147.

9. Belden C. Lane, *The Solace of Fierce Landscapes: Exploring Desert and Mountain Spirituality* (New York: Oxford University Press, 1998), 43.

10. Ibid., 44.

11. William Faulkner, *Requiem for a Nun* (New York: Random House, 1951; repr., New York: Vintage, 1975), 80.

12. Elizabeth Johnson, *Friends of God and Prophets: A Feminist Theological Reading of the Communion of Saints* (New York: Continuum, 1998), 1–2.

13. Ibid., 2.

14. Ibid., 167.

15. Sharon Welch, *A Feminist Ethic of Risk* (Minneapolis: Fortress Press, 1990), 154–55.

16. Kingsolver, *High Tide in Tucson*, 255.

17. Johnson, *Friends of God and Prophets*, 203.

18. Ibid., 205.

19. Ibid., 216, 217.

20. Ibid., 217.

21. Ibid.

Chapter 5

JESUS
God's Story of Love and Hope

And so we have reached the key question of our investigation: where does Jesus fit in all of this? Our journey so far has led us to new insights about how women construct their understanding of themselves, God, and the world. We know that a particular understanding of these three elements—self, God, and world—is necessary to every story of redemption, and undergirds a given story's shape and basic flow. By looking at the stories women tell about themselves, God, and the world, we have glimpsed the building blocks of a story of redemption that would resonate deep in the hearts of women. In the preceding chapters, we have seen that in their experience as mothers, women recognize that suffering is only part of the story, and they respond to suffering out of their commitment to a larger whole. We have seen them embrace the presence of God instead of longing for a God of violence and punitive power. Finally, we have opened our eyes to a new way of thinking about time and storytelling, a way that both emphasizes the flexibility of time and the possibility that women can take on the role of protagonists of history, thus shaping the stories in which we live. The redemption women seek, then, is marked by God's presence, by wholeness, and by a story that reshapes the meaning of the past. But the question remains: is what Jesus offers the same as what women are seeking? This is a significant—and scary—question: if the answer is no, then one of two miserable things is true. Either women as a group fundamentally misunderstand the basics of reality (who they are, who God is, and how the world works), or else what Christianity offers us will not, in the end, help us. Neither is an attractive option. Of course, it should be said that I am convinced that we don't have to make that choice—that the answer to the question about whether or not Jesus offers what women seek is a resounding *YES!* What women (and indeed, all people, women, men, and children) are seeking can be found in the person and story of Jesus of Nazareth. In this chapter, we will explore the Gospels together, in order to see how women's glimpses of redemption and redemptive hope find their fulfillment in the story of Jesus—the story God tells us about love, hope, and the truth at the heart of creation.

There are three key pieces to any consideration of who Jesus is for Christians today, and what his story means for us. We need to look at the doctrine of the incarnation: the fact that Jesus was God-made-flesh, come to live among us. We also need to look at Jesus' life and mission, and finally, at his passion and death. Each of these three elements links to the hopes and dreams of women as we have come to understand them in revealing and ultimately powerful ways. Just to hint at some of the ideas we will be discussing: the incarnation is the ultimate statement of God's presence; Jesus' life is marked by a compassion that draws us all toward a new understanding of human wholeness; and the story we tell of Jesus' passion and death transforms our understanding of God's involvement in our own suffering. And there is more, much more: the Gospel stories of Jesus are truly stories of love, hope, and promise. We will begin by looking at the incarnation, and thinking about what it can mean to follow a God who became a human being.

Incarnation

The story of Jesus is, of course, more than just a single story. We have four canonical Gospels, each of which tells a different story of Jesus' life, death, and new life in God. Moreover, there are still more Gospels—the Gospel of Mary, for example, and the Gospel of Thomas. Though not accepted by the church, these Gospels, too, add to the story of Jesus, if only by defining its outer limits, the point at which we say, "No, Jesus was *not* like that." Some scholars today speculate that we would be enriched by looking more carefully at the noncanonical Gospels (and this may well be true), but that would require some mountain climbing that our journey doesn't have to include right now.[1] Instead, we will stay on the more familiar paths marked out for us by Matthew, Mark, Luke, and John.

Each of the four Gospels included in the New Testament begins by defining Jesus' relationship to God as something special, something wonderful and new. This Jesus is not just another human being, nor is he merely a great prophet or teacher. Both Matthew and Luke tell marvelous stories of his birth, and Mark opens with his baptism, after which the heavens open so that God may declare, "You are my Son, the Beloved; with you I am well pleased" (Mark 1:11). Even more startlingly, John opens not with the birth or baptism of the man Jesus of Nazareth, but with the creation of the universe:

> In the beginning was the Word, and the Word was with God, and the Word was God. He was in the beginning with God. All things came into being through him, and without him not one thing came into being. What has come into being in him was life, and the life was the light of all people. . . . And the Word became flesh and lived among us. (John 1:1–4, 14)

Given this strong connection between God and Jesus in the Gospels, it may come as a surprise to realize that the earliest Christians probably didn't think about Jesus *as God* in the same way that we do. The doctrine of the Trinity didn't come of age until several hundred years after the death and resurrection of Jesus; and yet, as is evident in the openings of all four Gospels, there was a deep, if only partly articulated, sense of the profound connection between Jesus and his Abba from the time of the first Christian communities. This sense of connection, struggling for words to contain and define it, finally found theological expression in the idea of *incarnation*: that is, in the claim that Jesus was not simply God's son (by birth or baptism) but was in fact God; and more than that, was God become human, somehow both fully God and fully human.

The idea of incarnation is tremendously moving—and shocking. To claim that the infinite God who birthed the universe can be found in a single human life is nothing short of bizarre. That the single human life we're talking about is that of a brutally executed young man—not a king, not a hero, not someone the world might be willing to recognize as Infinite Power—is more shocking still. We are so accustomed to think of God as pure spirit, separate and distant from the struggling, hungry, often dirty flesh-and-blood lives we human beings live: how could God become one of us? And we are even more accustomed to associate greatness with power and might: how could the great God become incarnate in a poor peasant child living on the half-civilized edge of a long-ago empire? All our assumptions are overthrown. Yet the intuitions we drew forth from women's hopes and experiences are confirmed: it is not God's power we seek, but God's presence. And the wholeness revealed in the God-become-human serves to begin to heal the pernicious divisions we insist on making between body and spirit, God and people, weak and strong, history and today. Let us examine the idea of incarnation more carefully, looking at the openings of each of the four Gospels in turn, to see how this notion opens up in the same direction that women have been looking.

Matthew

There are ongoing scholarly debates about the historical accuracy of many elements of what we commonly call the Christmas story. More than that, the "story" we all know so well is actually two separate and very different stories, one told by Matthew and the other by Luke. There are no shepherds in Matthew and no wise men in Luke; an angel appears to Mary in Luke and to Joseph in Matthew; there is no census in Matthew and hence no journey to Bethlehem nor birth in a stable—Jesus was simply born at home in Bethlehem (his family moved to Nazareth after the flight to Egypt—of which there is no mention in Luke). We tend to deal with these differences by collapsing the two stories into one. We weave them together, with the angel appearing first to Mary and then to Joseph, and the shepherds arriving before the wise men. While historians and scholars wrestle with what is most likely to have "really" happened, our instinct to gather up the two stories into one actually makes sense, if we keep in mind that what we are after is *theological* information about God and God's relationship to Jesus, not historical data about events in first-century Israel. The precise details of history are more or less lost to us, but what the early Christian communities wanted to convey to us about Jesus and God is vibrantly, richly present in these stories. Moreover, if we're looking not for history but for what the early Christians wanted to tell us, then *all* the details of both stories, even when they're inconsistent or contradictory, become significant. We don't have to make the stories "work" or fit together; instead, we have to let ourselves be open to the wider truths toward which each element of each story leads us. The stories—like all Scripture—are rich and complex enough for a lifetime of reflection, and I would hope that you would return to them again and again during your journey. For now, however, I will focus on a few points raised by each story, keeping in mind that this is only the barest beginning of the kind of exploration that is possible. Let us look, then, first at Matthew, and then at Luke, considering carefully what each story tells us not only about Jesus, but about the God revealed in Jesus.

The Gospel of Matthew contains several of the central, familiar moments of the Christmas story: Joseph's dream encounter with an angel, the visit of the wise men, the flight to Egypt, and the massacre of the infants of Bethlehem. Yet Matthew also contains another significant part of the tale, one that is often overlooked in popular retellings. The Gospel of Matthew opens with a detailed genealogy that locates Jesus firmly within Israel's history, and portrays that history in a very pointed way, selecting one beginning point among several possibilities, and highlighting specific historical figures and events while ignoring others of equal moment. The choices Matthew made in presenting the genealogy of Jesus are significant, and tell us a lot about what Matthew wants us to know about Jesus, and about God's relationship with the people of Israel.

The genealogy begins with Abraham—but why there? Genesis names Abraham's father, and his father's father, and indeed traces his lineage back to Noah. And there's no reason to stop there, either, as another genealogical list traces the connections from Adam, the first man, all the way to Noah. In other words, it would have been possible to start Jesus' genealogy even further back in time—all the way back to the first human being, if Matthew had wanted to do that. But he didn't, even though the information was freely available. Why not? Why choose Abraham? If Jesus' genealogy began with Noah, we would associate him with the one righteous man who escaped the flood and began the world anew. If it began with Adam, we would associate him with the very beginning, with the first father of humanity. But to begin with Abraham means recalling God's promise to Abram (not Abraham yet): "Go from your country and your kindred and your father's house to the land that I will show you. I will make of you a great nation, and I will bless you, and make your name great, so that you will be a blessing" (Gen. 12:1–2). Naming Abraham as Jesus' ancestor means naming Jesus as an heir to that promise, and that blessing; it also makes the simple association in our minds between Jesus and the concepts of promise and blessing.

The genealogy has several other interesting features besides its choice of a beginning. It is divided into three parts: from Abraham to David, from David to the Babylonian exile, and from the exile to Jesus. The genealogy is structured to highlight both David and the exile, thus indicating that both were key events in Israel's history, and events that help us understand who Jesus was and is. Other events might have been emphasized—the Exodus, for example, or the giving of the Covenant—but Matthew chooses to point us toward David's kingship and the Babylonian exile. What can we learn from this? Certainly associating Jesus with Israel's most beloved king is significant, not only in recalling God's close and tender relationship with David, but because Israel was living in the hope that an heir of David would return, and restore Israel to its previous glory. More intriguing is the emphasis on the exile, yet that, too, fits in with the notion of God's promise and Israel's hope. Israel had come to interpret the end of the Babylonian exile and return to Jerusalem as a second Exodus—another stunningly powerful intervention by God into history on behalf of his beloved people. The exile was a symbol not only of how far Israel could fall when it strayed from the ways of God, but of God's faithfulness in the midst of human defeat and despair. Recalling how God rescued Israel from the Babylonian Empire at a point in history when Israel was being occupied by the Roman Empire was a clear reminder that God rescues his people from the depredations of great (human) powers.

Finally, the genealogy has a unique feature of special interest to women: this is not simply a list of fathers and sons. Surprisingly, several women make an appearance in the list of Jesus' ancestors. This is a strange thing for a biblical genealogy, and stranger still when one takes a close look at the women named here. They are not models of purity, wifely obedience, nor any "traditional" female virtues. Two are not even Jewish. Instead, each is a woman who played a key role in the history of Israel through defying convention, expectation, and the rules of appropriate sexual behavior. When Tamar's father-in-law violated her rights as a widow by refusing to marry her to his youngest son, she tricked him into fathering her children. Rahab was a foreign prostitute, but one who helped Joshua conquer Jericho. Ruth, another foreigner, claimed her rights as a widow with a little less trickery than Tamar but no less initiative, and thus became an ancestor of David. Finally, Bathsheba's adulterous entry into the history of Israel is proclaimed loudly in Matthew's blunt choice of words: "And David was the father of Solomon by the wife of Uriah" (Matt. 1:6). Through the genealogy, then, we see Jesus' ancestry shaped by women whose actions made them protagonists of history. We also see hints that a familiar, ongoing story (that of Israel's relationship with God) is about to have its meaning radically shifted by new events that change our understanding of the past. The history of Israel, so long focused on the hope for a (political, militarily powerful) messiah and an independent kingdom, is reshaped in the Christian story. Here we see a new interpretation of the history of Israel, one that leads to the proclamation of the presence of the Kingdom of God all around us, under the leadership not of a warrior-king, but a crucified one, resurrected by God.

Luke

Matthew's Christmas tale contains much more food for reflection, but for now our journey will turn to Luke's story of the birth of Jesus. There are two items of particular interest for us here, both involving angels: the Annunciation, and the appearance of angels to the shepherds near

Bethlehem. The Annunciation is of special interest to us because a woman, Mary, is at the heart of the story. Where Matthew tells the story by emphasizing the motivations and decisions made by Joseph (who was a good man, planned to divorce Mary quietly, dreamed of a message from God, and followed his instructions obediently), Luke focuses on Mary. Indeed, we learn far more about Mary here than we heard about Joseph in Matthew. Rather than receiving instructions in a dream, Mary has a full-blown encounter with the angel Gabriel. She speaks to the angel, questions him, and explicitly accepts her commission from God: "Let it be with me according to your word" (Luke 1:38). For centuries, Christians honored Mary primarily for her humility and obedience to God, but unquestioning obedience is not what this story portrays, nor is "humble" a particularly appropriate word to describe the woman who knew and celebrated the fact that "all generations will call me blessed; for the Mighty One has done great things for me, and holy is his name" (Luke 1:48–49). Our cultural expectations of a "good woman" shaped our understanding of Mary, and blinded us to her courage, her independence, and her boldness. We didn't expect to see those things in a woman, and so even when they were there, we called them by safer, more familiar names: "obedience" and "humility" and even "submissiveness." What a misreading! And what disrespect! Here was a child of thirteen or fourteen, clearly frightened by what is always in biblical terms a terrifying experience—an encounter with a messenger of the Lord—and she manages not only to hold her own enough to ask questions, but to make a deliberate statement of her intent to participate in a venture that she knew could cost her not only her reputation and her fiancé, but her life. An unmarried girl found pregnant could expect to be executed; that Mary is portrayed as calmly moving forward despite this risk demonstrates courage not many of us could claim to have. Moreover, when Mary's encounter with Gabriel is compared to Zechariah's (Gabriel announces the birth of John the Baptist to his father Zechariah before coming to Mary), a striking difference emerges: Zechariah never agreed to what was going to happen. He did not choose; he was told. Mary, on the other hand, assumed that she was being presented with a choice, not a command, and she chose. The idea that women are and must be protagonists of history, deeply involved in the shape of the world and of the story in which we live, could not be made more clear.

Angelic messengers are also on hand at the birth of Jesus, announcing the "good news of great joy" to nearby shepherds (Luke 2:10). Where Matthew tells us of wise men, whom we often portray as kings, greeting the holy child and doing homage to him, Luke focuses on people at the other end of the economic and political spectrum. Shepherds are not

known to be either wise or powerful, and their testimony is clearly not
something that would "frighten all Jerusalem," as did the words of the
wise men. What is going on here? It is one thing to proclaim that Gentiles
saw signs of the royalty of Jesus—that seems to fit with an overall theme
of those close to Jesus not recognizing who he really was. But why shepherds? Why would the announcement of the birth of the Messiah be given
to shepherds in their fields at night, and not to the priests of Jerusalem, or
to the wealthy and powerful, who might see in this new king one of their
own? The answer, of course, is clear when we look at the two stories
together: in Matthew, when the people of Jerusalem and the people of
power and wealth learned of the birth of Jesus, it did not fill them with
gratitude and hope, but with fear. They knew that their own power was
threatened. On the other hand, when the poor—the shepherds—were told
of the birth of the Messiah, they hastened to his side, to marvel and to tell
Mary and Joseph about the angels and what they had said. It was good
news for the shepherds; it was bad news for Herod. We need both these
stories; we need to know both these things to understand what Jesus
meant to people. To the poor and the outcast, his coming was good news.
To the powerful, it was threatening, and they responded with violence.

The Christmas story (more precisely, *stories*) told by Luke and Matthew,
then, tells us a lot about the incarnation, about God becoming human in
Jesus. But Mark and John also have something to say about the incarnation,
and their messages are not only radically different from Luke and Matthew's
birth stories, but wildly different from one another. We'll start with Mark.

Mark

The Gospel of Mark is the oldest gospel and the shortest. It begins not
with the birth of Jesus, but with the preaching of John the Baptist. John
"proclaimed a baptism of repentance for the forgiveness of sins" (Mark 1:4),
and also spoke of the One who was to come after him, baptizing not with
water, but with the Holy Spirit (Mark 1:8). Jesus, the One of whom John
spoke, is introduced in a few short verses. The richness packed in these few
words is difficult to overstate, and so we should examine the text as a whole:

> In those days Jesus came from Nazareth of Galilee and was baptized by
> John in the Jordan. And just as he was coming up out of the water, he saw
> the heavens torn apart and the Spirit descending like a dove upon him. And
> a voice came from heaven, "You are my Son, the Beloved; with you I am
> well pleased." And the Spirit immediately drove him out in the wilderness.
> (Mark 1:9–12)

In Mark, Jesus is publicly identified as the Son of God not at his birth but at his baptism. He is already an adult and about to embark on his mission of preaching and teaching: it is here that his Sonship is confirmed. This tells us that, at least in part, Sonship has to do with *doing* as well as *being*. It wasn't just that Jesus merely existed as the Son of God in the world; rather, he acted in a way that made that status real. His choice of what to do and with whom to identify made a difference. Later in this chapter we will consider Jesus' mission in detail; there we will see more clearly how the Son of God acts in the world. The important thing to remember here is that Mark reminds us that the incarnation is not just about the birth of a baby. It is not something that we should domesticate or trivialize by focusing too intently on the idea of God/Jesus as a helpless infant. Rather, the incarnation is something that makes all of Jesus' adult actions and choices resound with meaning, for *what Jesus is doing is who God is.*

John

The Gospel of John stands apart from all the others. It contains no parables and few miracles; instead, Jesus often speaks at great length in a difficult metaphorical, philosophical style. It is the gospel that is most firm and clear about Jesus' divinity. There are no obscure, mysterious hints here, but instead flat statements: "I am the light of the world" (8:12); "I am not of this world" (8:23); "I am the resurrection and the life" (11:25); "Before Abraham was, I am" (8:58). That last is the most forceful of all, since "I am" is the sacred name of God first revealed to Moses at the burning bush. Jesus' "I am" statements, his preaching style, and even the poetic prologue that speaks of the Word and the Light seem a strange break from earlier gospels, yet all three issues make sense if seen in terms of the biblical tradition of Sophia, or Wisdom.

Most of us think of the Old Testament as relentlessly patriarchal, with a male warrior God and male kings, priests, and prophets. The few women mentioned are often only there to have babies—they're rarely the star of the show. Ancient Israel is a man's world, run by a very male God. Yet as we saw in reading *A Weave of Women*, this is a rather mistaken impression. God's *Shekhinah*—the indwelling presence of God—is portrayed in female terms, and her abiding presence seems more central to people's day-to-day experience of God than long-ago tales of the Warrior God who destroyed the Egyptians. And it is not just the *Shekhinah* who is seen as God's presence in female guise: there is also Sophia, or Wisdom. Most Christians are unfamiliar with the depth and strength of the tradition of seeing God as Wisdom; but the authors of the Gospels, especially the Gospel of John, drew heavily on this understanding of who God is and how God interacts with human beings.

The one place many Christians have encountered this strong female figure is the book of Proverbs, yet even here we often misunderstand her role. We see her as an all-too-human contrast to the bad women of Proverbs; we assume that Wisdom is an idealized model for women, unlike the foolish woman who is "loud . . . [and] ignorant and knows nothing" (9:13) and the seductive woman, luring men away from the paths of righteousness (2:16–19). Yet Wisdom as portrayed in Proverbs is more than a good woman or even a good wife (see 31:10–31). Instead, she is a prophet; she is God's partner in creation; and she is One who calls the people to life in terms that are startlingly familiar to us: "Come, eat of my bread and drink of the wine I have mixed. Lay aside immaturity, and live, and walk in the way of insight" (9:5–6). Is it any wonder that some early Christians thought of Jesus as Wisdom?

Let us examine the biblical portrayal of Wisdom in more depth. As the book of Proverbs opens, Wisdom is portrayed as a prophet, calling out to the people of Israel, trying to lure them into the ways of God: "Wisdom cries out in the street; in the squares she raises her voice . . . 'How long, O simple ones, will you love being simple? . . . Give heed to my reproof; I will pour out my thoughts to you; I will make my words known to you'" (1:22–23). She claims that her words are truth (8:7), and that she walks in the way of righteousness and justice (8:20). Like other prophets, she both rages and promises, lures and condemns. She is frustrated that people ignore her, yet promises that "I love those who love me, and those who seek me diligently find me" (8:17). In the midst of a prophetic tradition that always recognized that kings rule only by God's leave, and that their justice is a reflection of God's, she declares boldly, "By me kings reign, and rulers decree what is just" (8:15). She cries out to the simple in words that recall to us words spoken by Jesus (hundreds of years later): "Come, eat of my bread and drink of the wine I have mixed. Lay aside immaturity, and live" (9:5–6). She is a figure of strength, like all prophets who boldly preach the word of God to a world more deaf than hearing, and like all prophets, she claims an intimacy with God and deep understanding of the justice of God.

Yet Wisdom goes further than any other prophet. She is not merely a chosen mouthpiece to whom God speaks in a special way; instead, she declares, "The LORD created me at the beginning of his work, the first of his acts of long ago. . . . Before the mountains had been shaped, before the hills, I was brought forth" (8:22, 25). So Wisdom is the first-born of creation—and even more than that:

When he established the heavens, I was there,
When he drew a circle on the face of the deep,
When he made firm the skies above,
When he established the fountains of the deep,
When he assigned to the sea its limit,
So that the waters might not transgress his command,
When he marked out the foundations of the earth,
Then I was beside him, like a master worker;
And I was daily his delight, rejoicing before him always,
Rejoicing in his inhabited world and delighting in the human race.
(8:27–31)

When John tells us that the Word "was in the beginning with God. All things came into being through him, and without him not one thing came into being" (1:2–3), the echoes of the Wisdom tradition could not be clearer. Yet why does John say "Word," and not "Wisdom"? If it is Wisdom who offers us bread and wine, who created the world with God, and who calls us to walk in the ways of God, why doesn't John explicitly identify Jesus and Wisdom? Why not say, "In the beginning was Wisdom, and Wisdom was with God, and Wisdom was God"?

Scholars have debated this issue, and, sadly, it appears that the key issue was the female character of Sophia. While the influence of the Jewish Wisdom tradition is dramatically present throughout the Gospels, epistles, and early Christian hymns, by the time the Gospel of John was written, Christianity was being shaped by a deeply patriarchal (and often misogynist) Greek culture and philosophy. The author of the Gospel of John was living in a culture that was deeply convinced that it was not fitting to associate God with anything female, and so substituting the masculine word *Logos* (reason) for the feminine *Sophia* (wisdom) was a change that made all too much sense. Now, it is possible to see that as either disheartening for women today who know that femaleness is no more distant from God than maleness, or as *encouraging* because—unlike much of the later tradition— the earliest Christian communities saw no reason that femaleness and God should be set in opposition to one another. Theologian Elizabeth Johnson tells us that "the tradition of personified Wisdom plays a foundational role in the development of Christology, and some of the most profound christological assertions in the New Testament are made in its categories."[2] In other words, when early Christians tried to talk about what Jesus meant to them and who he was in relationship to God, the words and ideas they used came from the tradition of talking about God as Wisdom personified. Early Christians spoke of Jesus as Wisdom's child, or Wisdom's messenger.

By the end of the first century, people went even further and spoke of Jesus "as divine Sophia herself."[3] Unfortunately, as Christianity became more embedded in a Greek culture that saw everything female as bad, or at least as obviously "less than" everything male, there was no possible way to continue to speak of God in female terms. Moreover, this shift away from Sophia-language was accompanied by a shift away from women being active in Christian ministry (or protagonists of Christian history). Elizabeth Johnson is all too blunt about what happened:

> Christian reflection before John had not found it difficult to associate Jesus Christ with Sophia, including not only the risen and exalted Christ but even the historical Jesus of the ministry. Insofar as the gender of Sophia was a factor in her replacement by the Logos in the Prologue [of John], it was coherent with the broader shift in the Christian community toward more patriarchal ecclesial structures and the blocking of women from ministries in which they had earlier participated. In other words, the suppression of Sophia is a function of the growth of sexism in the Christian communities.[4]

It is tremendously sad to think that we lost a significant part of our Christian tradition because people couldn't bear to think of God in female terms. On the other hand, women today should be deeply encouraged by the fact that the first Christians had wider and more flexible imaginations than many who came after them (and many who are alive today!). For them, it was not a problem to proclaim that "Jesus Christ is the human being Sophia became,"[5] and to live in awe and gladness that such a thing could come to be. After all, Sophia—whom they had known as "sister, mother, female beloved, chef and hostess, preacher, judge, liberator, establisher of justice" and even as the Torah itself—was the presence of God among them, and the route to God in their lives.[6] That she should appear as a human being just like them was a tremendous gift from God, and an affirmation of God's love for human beings.

Thus, John's Gospel presents us with the most powerful testimony yet of the significance of the incarnation. The invisible God has become present and "pitched his tent among us"[7] in a way that emphasizes not his dominating power but his reassuring and comforting presence. Come to me, all you who are weary, says Jesus; Come to me, you simple, says Wisdom. Jesus as Wisdom, the Beloved and delight of God, beckons us forward in our journey toward a new kind of life. To discover what that kind of life might be, we turn to a discussion of Jesus' mission and ministry. It is here that Jesus shows us how to live in the presence of God, under the Reign of God, even in the midst of the struggles and suffering around us.

Proclaiming God's Reign

There are great debates going on today in Christology, or scholarship about Jesus. Theologians and biblical scholars have begun to make use of historical and archaeological evidence about all aspects of the ancient Mediterranean world in order to illuminate Jesus' situation (and the situation of early Christian communities) as clearly as possible. Of course, this is no easy task, and there are many gaps in what we can know. Much evidence has been lost, and even if we had all the documents and artifacts imaginable, it would still be difficult to drop our twenty-first-century assumptions and patterns of thought and truly attempt to enter into the world of first-century, Roman-occupied Palestine. Hence, arguments rage about how we should best understand Jesus and his mission. In the midst of scholarly disputes, however, theologian Monika Hellwig tells us that most scholars agree on two key points about Jesus' preaching: it focused on the "hope and expectation and promise of God's reign" among us, and it rang with "a clarity and confidence that did not come from book learning."[8] Both of these points are important. We need to understand the reign of God that Jesus promised, and we need to understand Jesus' confidence in proclaiming that God's reign was here among us.

Hellwig says that scholars agree that Jesus' preaching was powerful but not rooted in "book learning," which at the time would have meant years of Scripture study. Now, it is certainly true that years of study and immersion in books can sometimes lead people to speak and write in a way that obscures far more than it illuminates, but I don't think that Hellwig here is critiquing scholars for their lack of clarity and/or charisma. After all, it is more than possible to preach with clarity, confidence, *and* a theological education—Martin Luther King Jr.'s speeches and writings are proof of that—and so I think Hellwig is not here critiquing scholars, but making a different and important point. Jesus, as far as anyone can determine, did not come from the wealthy, educated elite. He was a peasant, and thus never had the chance to spend his youth poring over the Scriptures, coming to love God through deep and long engagement with God's word. Instead, although the Scriptures were part of his life and worship, Jesus' source of confidence and clarity lay elsewhere. That source, scholars believe, was Jesus' "Abba-experience," his experience of profound intimacy with God.

The Gospel writers tell us that Jesus called God "Abba," a term we often translate as Father but which is better rendered "Papa" or "Daddy," for it is a child's early attempt at speech, not an adult's formal address. This is important, for a child has a much different relationship with Papa than an adolescent or adult does with Father. Papa is the one who holds you close when the monsters frighten you; Father frowns if you bring home lousy grades. Papa's face lights up with a smile when he sees you, and sometimes he throws you up in the air or spins you in circles, making you squeal in delight while he laughs for sheer joy. Father, on the other hand, even when he loves you deeply, is more serious, more concerned about what is appropriate and how to prepare you to face The Real World. I have perhaps pushed the stereotypes too far—there are many adults who have a close and loving relationship with their fathers—but the point is, there's a simplicity, joy, and untroubled intimacy in a child's relationship with Papa, and it's that kind of relationship that Jesus apparently had with God. What an amazing thing! Love, joy, and trust—without fear. In our culture and most others (including that of Jesus), a trace or sometimes a large helping of fear often becomes part of a child's relationship with the father sooner or later, since the father's role in the family is that of Enforcer ("just wait until your father gets home!"), Law-Giver, and Judge. Similarly, we often think of God as the ultimate enforcer (who hands out punishments and sentences people to hell), the first law-giver (the ten commandments, for instance) and our final judge (the Last Judgment). In contrast to this understanding of God and God's role in our lives, Jesus lived and preached a relationship of love and trust between Papa and his beloved child. The idea of this sort of relationship is wonderful—and frightening. Dare we claim such intimacy with the Creator of all things? Isn't that rather bold? Presumptuous? After all, could it really be possible that God would love us like that? Besides, we've done plenty of things in our lives that we know perfectly well deserve punishment, judgment, and condemnation. For most of us, to have the trust that Jesus had in his Abba requires a leap of faith and courage that we're afraid to make.

Most of the people to whom Jesus preached lacked that same courage, and Jesus' preaching and teaching were aimed at trying to change that. Jesus preached the reign of God: that is, he proclaimed to all who would listen that the world God had dreamed for us was within our grasp. In his storytelling, healing, eating practices, and offers of forgiveness, Jesus reached out to the poor and to sinners, telling them and showing them that God's reign was real, and was being born among them. Some believed, and followed him. Others believed, but didn't dare follow. Still others heard and grew angry: if God's reign were truly to come, what would happen to their power and privilege? Jesus preached not only a relationship with God that was radically trusting, but a resulting relationship with others that was characterized first and foremost by compassion, by an imitation of God's compassion for all God's people. The reign of God is among you,

Jesus told us; therefore be compassionate as your Father is compassionate. The Jewish tradition had long spoken of the coming reign of God, when the righteous would be vindicated and all our most treasured dreams would come to pass. Like Jesus, the tradition had even insisted that if people lived now as if the reign of God were present, then they would experience the reign of God in their lives. More than anyone else had before or since, Jesus lived within that ideal.[9] And his mission was to draw others into that way of life, that acknowledgment of God's lordship, that position of radical trust, love, and compassion.

It should not be surprising that the wholeness women seek finds its fullest expression in the kind of life Jesus lived and the kind of life he calls his followers to live. Where women seek to attend to the demands of suffering while looking toward a larger story that embraces and transforms suffering, Jesus' actions, too, addressed suffering with compassion while looking beyond it to the reign of God. Jesus addressed the pain of hunger and social exclusion through the meals he ate and the people with whom he chose to share food and drink. He forgave those suffering from their sins, and healed many suffering from physical ailments. He even sought to heal those suffering from an impoverished understanding of God by luring them toward new ideas and new life in his storytelling. In all his actions, he was living in the reign of God and calling other people to live there with him. We need to look at each of the four main ways Jesus acted to bring about the reign of God: his offers of forgiveness, his healing of the sick, his sharing of food with others, and his storytelling (parables). Each of these speaks to women's search for a redemption that does not negate suffering, nor parts of our lives or ourselves, but instead embraces all in a new story and new life that transforms what has come before.

Curing the Sick

First let us explore Jesus' healing ministry. Stories of miraculous healings abound in the Gospels: Jesus healed a man with a withered arm, a bent woman, a paralyzed man, several blind men, a group of ten lepers, and (among many others) our old friend, the woman with the hemorrhage. He also healed people who did not request healing themselves: a Roman centurion asked that Jesus heal a servant, and a foreign woman asked that he heal her daughter. The healings not only demonstrate Jesus' concern for those suffering physically, they also serve as a powerful signal to Jews at the time that the kingdom of God had come to birth among them. Recall the question John's disciples asked Jesus: "John the Baptist has sent us to you to ask, 'Are you the one who is to come, or are we to wait for another?'" (Luke 7:20) Jesus did not answer with an account of his relationship with God, nor a simple "Yes!" Instead, he replied, "Go and tell John what you have seen and heard: the blind receive their sight, the lame walk, the lepers are cleansed, the deaf hear, the dead are raised, the poor have good news brought to them" (Luke 7:22). Jesus knew—and all who heard him knew, and John would know—that the great prophet Isaiah had spoken of the redemption of Israel from bondage in Babylon and the restoration of God's kingship over his people as follows:

> Then the eyes of the blind shall be opened, and the ears of the deaf
>   unstopped;
> Then the lame shall leap like a deer, and the tongue of the speechless sing
>   for joy.
> For waters shall break forth in the wilderness, and streams in the desert . . .
> And the ransomed of the LORD shall return, and come to Zion with singing;
> Everlasting joy shall be upon their heads; they shall obtain joy and gladness,
> And sorrow and sighing will flee away. (Isaiah 35:5–6, 10)

This ancient hope that God would redeem Israel from a very concrete enemy, the Babylonians, had gradually become not only a memory of what God did accomplish (the Israelites were freed to return to Jerusalem) but a promise of what would happen in the future when no one but God reigned. When asked if he was "the one who is to come," the promised messiah who would rule with justice, compassion, and righteousness, Jesus said, in essence, "Look around you: what has been promised is beginning to come true. God's reign is breaking forth in the world."

The healings Jesus performed not only recalled prophecies of what life under God's reign would be like, they also made some very clear points about what human wholeness is and should be, and how important it is. For example, when the Canaanite woman asked Jesus to heal her daughter, he initially refused, claiming that he had come only to save God's people Israel, not foreigners. But she was not one to give up easily, and argued with him: "Yes, Lord, yet even the dogs eat the crumbs that fall from their masters' table" (Matt. 15:27). Jesus seemed startled by her reply, and acknowledged its justice by granting her request. "And her daughter was healed instantly," Matthew tells us (15:28). What is especially interesting about this story is that it is about a foreigner—indeed, an enemy of the Israelites. Some people use this healing story to remind us of the importance of persistence in prayer, and others have argued that its inclusion in the gospels implies that Jesus was open to learning new things (even from women!) as his ministry developed. However, there's another significant point to make here, one directly related to the theme of wholeness. All of us are God's people: the human race is one whole, not to be divided into God's people and "others," especially not "enemies of God." The Canaanite woman knelt before Jesus and said, "Lord, help me" (15:25), and she was helped. The circle of salvation was widening: once seen as a promise primarily for Israel (though it always included a renewal of creation), we see in the gospels and in this healing story especially that God offers wholeness and redemption to all.

Breaking Bread with Sinners

The second thing Jesus did to introduce the reign of God to people is eat with them. This is a more significant gesture than we might at first realize. Sharing a meal is not a trivial event, much as our tendency towards "grabbing a quick bite" might suggest. Job candidates are often warned that lunch is a not-so-hidden part of the interview, and missteps there can cost you the position for which you seemed so qualified. Closer to home, there's a big difference between meeting your potential in-laws for the first time and being invited to Thanksgiving dinner: being included in a family meal and family celebration is a milestone that many people recognize, if only by how much stress the thought can trigger. Being invited to Thanksgiving dinner—or Christmas, or Easter, or a meal celebrating a birthday—is a marker of being included in the family, and as such is not just about food but about acceptance, love, and identity.

In Jesus' time and culture, it wasn't just major family celebrations or business luncheons, but all meals that made a statement about inclusion and social identity. The people with whom you would or would not eat demonstrated to others your social status and degree of religious observance. The society in which Jesus lived was a "purity society," one that was organized around strict separation of things and people that were pure from those things and people deemed impure, unclean, or "dirty."[10] Those who were pure were holy, like God. God was of course the ultimate definition of holiness—and therefore purity—and any sort of impurity or uncleanness meant a separation from God. This is an important point, and a strange one to our way of thinking, so I want to make it very clear: it was not just doing things that were *morally* wrong that could separate you from God. You could also find yourself at a distance from God because of physical contact with something unclean (like a dead body) or because of something physically "wrong" with you (including being sick—lepers were unclean—but also including childbirth and menstruation, which made you unclean for specified periods of time). We can still see echoes of this ancient association of holiness and purity in the notion that sin is a "stain" on the soul. Recall, too, sayings such as "cleanliness is next to godliness" and our continuing inclination to keep what is holy/pure separate from things we see as dirty or impure. An example of this final point would be the outcry several years ago over a painting of the Virgin Mary covered with elephant dung: the association of the pure Virgin with the excrement of an animal absolutely enraged many people. It's clear that the idea of sin and the idea of dirtiness, or impurity, are still linked in our minds, though not with the same strength as in ancient times.

Despite these lingering remnants of the association of purity and holiness, overall our society does not conceive of holiness in this way, and the rules of purity often seem oddly arbitrary to us. For example, almost no one today would assume that touching a dead body would separate you from God, nor would we use the term "sinner" to describe funeral directors merely because they are in constant contact with the dead. Yet in Jesus' day, contact with a dead body made one impure, just as blood, bleeding, giving birth, or being physically maimed made one unclean and unfit for a decent person to eat with. Thus Jesus' consistent choices not only to associate with but actually to eat with "tax collectors and sinners" (Luke 7:34) was a radical statement. By eating with the poor, the outcast, and the unclean, Jesus was indicating that he accepted them, that he welcomed them, and that they were welcome in the reign of God he preached. Surprisingly, God's reign was not reserved for the pure. Instead, it was open to all! This open table fellowship was such a significant marker of what it meant to be a follower of Jesus that it was incorporated into the central way Christians have of remembering Jesus: celebrating the Eucharist. The Eucharist celebrated by early Christians was not only a memorial of the Last Supper but a continuation of Jesus' insistence on open table fellowship; all ate together, Jew and Gentile, male and female, slave and free, in a way that would have been impossible under normal social rules. The wholeness of sharing a meal together overcame the divisions and separations imposed by the cultural rules of the wider society; the wholeness envisioned in the reign of God shone forth in this gathering together of all kinds of people.

Forgiving the Penitent

The third thing Jesus did to proclaim the arrival of the reign of God was freely offer forgiveness to people. Jesus was clearly aware of how an awareness of sin could cripple people, sometimes literally. That is one way to understand his cure of the paralyzed man whose friends lowered him through a hole in the roof in order to get close to Jesus (Luke 5:17–26). When Jesus saw the man, his first words were not about his paralysis, but about forgiveness: "Friend, your sins are forgiven you" (Luke 5:20). It is only when people murmur against such a bold declaration ("Who can forgive sins but God alone?" they ask [Luke 5:21]) that Jesus goes on to command the forgiven man to stand up and walk.

Forgiveness addresses our inner brokenness in profound ways. It is, of course, central to what most of us believe about Jesus: through him, we are forgiven. Being forgiven is a profoundly freeing experience. Often when we feel guilty or shamed, we cannot recognize ourselves as loveable, and certainly not as beloved of God. To be forgiven is to have that burden lifted. Even more importantly, forgiveness is a confirmation of ongoing relationship, and refusing forgiveness means ending a relationship, usually with bitterness. Refusing to forgive is often the greatest statement we can make about the depth of the wrong that has been done to us; we use it as a sign of complete rejection not only of an action but of the person who performed the action. When Jesus offers us forgiveness, he confirms that God is still in relationship with us, despite our sins. We have not been cast out, even if we feel we deserve to be. Through Jesus' persistent and generous offers of forgiveness, we learn that we cannot lose God's love; his forgiveness is always being offered, even before we ask.

Telling New Stories

Finally, Jesus tried to show people that the reign of God had arrived—and that it looked much different not only from the reign of imperial Rome, but also from the reign of any earthly power—by telling stories. Jesus' parables were pointedly directed at overturning people's everyday assumptions, and their power came from the surprising way in which he confronted his listeners' expectations and unexamined beliefs. He was working to push their imaginations in a new direction, in order that they begin to see how God was already working among them. As our own journey is about healing our imaginations, we, too, need to pay attention to the parables Jesus told, and to the world he created in their telling. A closer look at three parables should enable us to see their relationship to the reign of God, and to our ongoing theme of women's desire to look toward the wholeness of things.

First, let us consider the parable of the Good Shepherd, found both in Luke and Matthew. Interestingly enough, Jesus told this parable in response to the charge that he "welcomes sinners and eats with them" (Luke 15:2). Respectable people couldn't understand why Jesus would behave in such a way, and in response, Jesus offered them a story. He did not argue with them, nor offer a philosophical or theological justification for his behavior. Instead, he tried to point their imaginations in a new direction:

> Which one of you, having a hundred sheep and losing one of them, does not leave the ninety-nine in the wilderness and go after the one that is lost until he finds it? When he has found it, he lays it on his shoulders and rejoices. And when he comes home, he calls together his friends and neighbors, saying to them, "Rejoice with me, for I have found my sheep that was lost." Just so, I tell you, there will be more joy in heaven over one sinner who repents than over ninety-nine righteous persons who need no repentance. (Luke 15:4–7)

The image of God as a shepherd would have been familiar to Jesus' listeners: it was used by Isaiah (40:11), Ezekiel (34:11–16), and of course in the psalms. "The Lord is my shepherd, I shall not want" (Ps. 23:1) begins the most famous of all the psalms. Knowing that this image of God would resonate deeply with his listeners, Jesus used it to try to widen their understanding of God's actions in the world. "Why eat with sinners?" is another way of saying, "Don't you know that God has rejected these people and you should, too?" And so Jesus' story is a gentle reminder that God is more interested in pursuing the lost than in punishing them. This is a startling depiction of God for those raised with the understanding that God, whose holiness and purity separates him radically from everything impure, celebrates with the righteous and rejects the sinner. The most interesting thing here, of course, is that Jesus is taking on one image of God—as distant, pure, and perfect—by introducing another quite familiar image: God as the shepherd who seeks the lost and strengthens the weak (Ezek. 34:16), gathering the lambs in his arms (Isa. 40:11). In some ways, Jesus seems to be saying, "You know the answer to your question already, you've just forgotten. Yes, God is holy . . . but that doesn't stop God from tending his flock." God's holiness is not separation, it is compassion. Interestingly, this image of God does not so much overturn a conventional hierarchy as throw it out altogether: Jesus does not claim that sinners are close to God and the righteous are far away. Rather, he acknowledges that there is joy in heaven for the righteous, but *more joy* when a sinner repents. It's not about drawing strict lines between winners and losers (the pure and the stained), but trying to cajole everyone possible into the winning category.

Finally, Jesus' story insists that sin—wandering away from God—is not the last word in the story of our relationship with God. Just like the mothers of *Beloved*, who attended to the immediate needs of suffering without making suffering the star of the show, God attends to the problem of sin without letting it become the key determinant of someone's fate. Rather, the focus is on God and God's actions, and in God's loving pursuit of the straying sheep. Certainly people can choose to resist and reject the pursuit of God, but Jesus is reminding us that our sin does not mean that God has already rejected *us*. If we wander off, God does not say "Good riddance" and care more tenderly for the sheep still with him, but instead follows us, rescues us, and rejoices with us. The story we tend to tell is that of sin determining who wins or loses God's love; the wider story that Jesus is calling us toward is that of God's love for all of humanity.

Next, consider the parable of the Good Samaritan. Again, this story tells us about God's salvation and God's love, and who will receive it and who will not. Again, Jesus topples our expectations. Recall that the parable opens not with the man traveling from Jerusalem to Jericho, but with a question about salvation: "What must I do to inherit eternal life?" asked a lawyer. Jesus turns the question back on him, asking, "What is written in the law?" The lawyer answers, "You shall love the Lord your God with all your heart, and with all your soul, and with all your strength, and with all your mind; and your neighbor as yourself" (Luke 10:27). Jesus acknowledges that this is right, and adds, "Do this, and you will live." But the lawyer—not a lawyer in our sense, but rather someone deeply learned in the Scriptures, also called the laws of Moses—pushes the question further. After all, this is how deeper understanding of the laws of Moses comes about, through questions, answers, and discussions with learned rabbis (Christians who tend to see faith as something that should never be questioned have really missed out on the opportunity to deepen and strengthen their understanding of their faith and their God; we could learn a lot from the Jewish tradition of persistent questioning). The lawyer asks Jesus, "Who is my neighbor?" and it is in answer to this question that Jesus tells the story of the man robbed and beaten, and the Samaritan who cares for him.

The context for this story is once again the purity laws: contact with a dead person makes one impure. Thus the priest and Levite have good reason to avoid a man "half-dead" (Luke 10:30); if they can't tell from a distance whether he is dead or alive, it's probably best to avoid him altogether. Touching a corpse renders a person unclean for seven days, and the unclean cannot serve at God's temple. In the common understanding of the time, then, those who wanted to serve God *had* to stay away from this half-dead man. They were choosing faithful service to God over the possibility (not even the certainty) of mere service to a human being, and surely God is more important than a human being, especially when you don't even know if this person is a terrible sinner, who was robbed and beaten because God's love and protection weren't surrounding him at a time of need. We are so used to thinking of the priest and Levite as selfish hypocrites; we need to take the time to look at things from their point of view, and from the point of view of Jesus' audience. Only then will we truly understand the strange and radical thought that Jesus was proposing. By insisting that the Samaritan had behaved "like a neighbor," Jesus is telling us that the Samaritan is the one fulfilling God's requirements for salvation. Attending to the needs of others is more important than being ritually pure in order to serve God; indeed, attending to the human needs of others *is* serving God. Compassion, not purity, is the key.

Compassion was at the heart of what Jesus was doing and talking about and practicing in his healing, forgiveness, eating practices, and in his storytelling, "Be compassionate, as God is compassionate," he told his followers, making a radical substitution for the more familiar, "Be holy as God is holy." The understanding of holiness at the time implied a strict system of separations: compassion, on the other hand, asked instead for one to recognize connection.

Finally, I would like to look at a brief parable, so short as to be easily overlooked. "To what should I compare the kingdom of God?" Jesus asks. "It is like yeast that a woman took and mixed in with three measures of flour until all of it was leavened" (Luke 13:20–21). If the kingdom is the yeast, then the image of God presented here is that of a Bakerwoman God, stirring just a tiny bit of the kingdom into the sprawling sinful world, and then watching the world transform under the influence of the living, growing kingdom. It's a wonderful image and links God's work explicitly with the work of feeding us, and the work of preparing food—the work, in other words, of mothers.

Surprisingly enough—especially to those of us who enjoy baking—the comparison of God's kingdom to yeast would have made Jesus' audience quite uncomfortable. Again, this goes back to purity issues. Yeast makes things swell up, and since corpses swell up, the image of yeast was often used to refer to corruption or uncleanness.[11] Here again we see Jesus saying that purity is not as important as the practical issues of caring for one another: indeed, the kingdom is like yeast, not because it is an image of corruption, but because it is a key ingredient in creating one of life's necessities—bread.

Jesus' life and mission were clearly oriented toward compassion, toward showing us a new way to live. Living under the reign of God as Jesus understood it meant basing one's actions not on the separations implied in traditional understandings of holiness, but in the inclusions and community called for in acts of kindness, compassion, and mercy. There was room here for everyone: uncleanness and sin could still be attended to, but they were part of the larger whole of God's dominion. This is a wonderful vision, but it's important to remember that it was *not* a rejection of Judaism, nor of Jewish understandings of God. Instead, both these traditions—holiness and compassion—existed in the Judaism of Jesus' time, and *they both still exist in Christianity today*. We often find ourselves pulled between these two poles: we believe in God's justice, and so we want the cruel and the greedy and the vicious punished; and we believe in God's mercy, so we know that forgiveness and love are always available. It is often difficult to accept Jesus' teachings of forgiveness and inclusion for all (does God really love the people who planned and executed the horrible crimes of 9/11?). And so, despite Jesus' teachings, there has often been a strong desire in Christian communities to separate from "the world," which is seen as an arena of darkness, a place where things are corrupt, or impure. We need to remember that it was not simply "those people long ago" who focused too much on rules and too little on mercy; rather, we need to recognize *ourselves* as among those who assume that God rewards the well-behaved and rejects the sinner! Jesus consistently shows us that God is the One who cares tenderly for the sick, the sinner, and the outcast; in today's terms, perhaps, we might say the AIDS victim, the drug dealer, and the illegal immigrant. The reign of God welcomes all of these: indeed, the wholeness we yearn for can never be complete without their presence. This can be quite difficult to accept, but the God who offers us food, forgiveness, and healing offers it to everyone. That is, after all, what wholeness is all about.

Passion, Death, and Resurrection

And here we are at last, confronting the mystery and terror of Jesus' passion and death. These terrible events lie at the heart of Christian faith. There is no way around them. We cannot comfort ourselves by staying with the lovely stories of Jesus' birth and preaching, focusing only on when things were going well, when his life was teaching us with its beauty and power. For that beauty ended in horror, and whatever power he demonstrated over sickness and death for others seemed to vanish when his own pain and death were imminent. It is easy to talk of Jesus' incarnation and his preaching toward wholeness, revealing God's presence among us. It is easy to speak of his life—his preaching and storytelling, his healings, and the meals he shared with friends and strangers alike—and make connections to the wholeness women seek, and to the comforting God who stands with them. Yet there is more to the story, and we cannot ignore it.

Jesus' passion and death, of course, are the reason why our understanding of him reeks of blood. This is where our images of sacrifice came from, and our tortured grasping after the idea that perhaps suffering can be pleasing to God, can result in good somehow. The crucifixion had to mean something, and to see it as a dramatic ransom, a final payment for sin, a sacrifice to end all sacrifice—all these things made sense and still make sense. This is the problem: the bloodthirsty story that Christians tell about Jesus is the best way we've got to talk about his death, which is the part that needs explaining most of all. We don't need stories to tell us why he lived; we can simply celebrate that. But we do need a story to make sense of his death: how on earth could this have happened? How could his life have ended like this? The oldest parts of the Gospels are the passion narratives; when the early Christians started telling stories about Jesus, and writing down what they absolutely had to remember, the first things they wrote down were the tales of his final hours. That was what had made the biggest impression, that was what needed the catharsis of storytelling, that was what had to be passed down, what could never be forgotten.

We have to respect this. The magnitude of the trauma faced by early Christians can never be minimized. They discovered God living among them, and then he was brutally murdered. Who can cope with that? The stories they scrambled after to make sense of it need to be honored . . . and yet, and yet. Again we come back to the problem of how stories work: we have facts, and we attach meanings and motivations to those facts in an effort to build a plot out of the chaos of our lives. We need to remember that the early Christians struggled so hard to "emplot" the death of Christ into a story that made sense that they told lots of stories about how and why it happened: they never settled on a single, definitive account. The story was—and remains—far too huge and complex to be captured by any human storytelling ability. And so I'd like to reflect a bit on why the stories we have aren't enough. I don't want to throw them out; they've meant too much to too many people for far too long to do that, but I want to discuss why we need more attempts to understand what happened and suggest a few stories to add to our repertoire. The passion and death of Jesus are enormous events, events that no one can ever truly grasp in their entirety. As Christians, we must try, of course. I'd like to suggest that we widen our view. We need to understand that there are several ways to tell this story, and to acknowledge that different ways to tell the story will "work" for different people, and even for the same people at different points in their lives—*and that's okay.* The wideness of God has room for us all.

Why Did He Die?

To start with, I think we can agree that the simple pronouncement "Jesus came to die for our sins" glosses over far too much that's deeply significant about Jesus, and what we have learned about God through Jesus. It is a simple formula but ultimately, too simplistic to be of much use. The God of life did not appear among us to show us death: we are all too familiar with that phenomenon, and anyway, Jesus did far more than just die. The passion narratives may be the oldest, but they are not the only narratives we have of Jesus. Those who knew him wanted us to know much more about him than the fact that he died.

Yet we are still left with the question, Why did he die? Why not live? Why not come among us and *stay*? Couldn't he have continued on, preaching and healing for years, gathering more people to him and to God, helping more and more people see and know love? If Israel was simply too dangerous a place to stay, he could have wandered the Mediterranean as Paul did a few decades later. Or perhaps he could have simply disappeared one day, vanished back into Eternity, as we are told Elijah did, riding a chariot to heaven. Surely there must have been other options!

But perhaps there really weren't any other options, not if Jesus was really about being the presence and person of God in our midst. After all, there was nothing truly surprising about Jesus' crucifixion; he'd been disturbing some very powerful people for quite a long time, in an age that had never heard of free speech and was all too familiar with public executions for reasons both large and small. The Romans, who occupied and ruled Israel during Jesus' lifetime, ran a shockingly brutal empire—something most of us don't even realize, having been taught that the great Roman Empire brought good roads, aqueducts, and "civilization" to much of the ancient world. Certainly their achievements in art and architecture were stunning and deserve to be celebrated, but we would do well to pay attention, too, to the cost of those trappings of civilization. Scholar Richard Horsley describes the character of the Roman Empire at the time of Jesus as follows:

> The initial Roman conquest of new peoples often entailed devastation of the countryside, burning of villages, pillage of towns, and slaughter and enslavement of the populace. The Romans then reacted with brutal reconquest and often outright genocide even to minor breaches of treaty and other threats to the international order they had imposed. . . . After viewing the horrific scene of human and animal corpses littering a city destroyed by the Romans, the historian Polybius wrote: "It seems to me

that they do this for the sake of terror." Deterrence by terrorism was practiced by Roman warlords and emperors throughout their imperial domination: "It was traditional; it was the Roman way."

. . . The Roman generals and governors assigned to Judea and Galilee
repeatedly used crucifixion as a means of terrorizing the populace, presumably to deter further resistance. In retaliation for the widespread revolt in
4 B.C.E., around the time Jesus was born, the Roman general Varus, after
burning towns and devastating the countryside, scoured the hills for rebels
and eventually had about two thousand men crucified.[12]

Despite such brutality, Jews continued to resist the Roman occupation
throughout Jesus' lifetime and beyond. The scattered resistance and subsequent violent repression continued until the great revolt of the years
66–70, which ended when the Romans sacked Jerusalem and destroyed
the Temple. This was right around the time when the Gospels were written; we would do well to remember the chaos and war that were their
background. This, for example, is a contemporary description of what
happened to people who attempted to flee Jerusalem when the Romans
were besieging the city:

They were accordingly beaten and subjected to torture of every description . . . and then crucified opposite the walls. Some five hundred or more
were captured daily. . . . [The Roman general] Titus hoped that the spectacle might induce the Judeans to surrender for fear that continued resistance would involve them in a similar fate. The soldiers out of rage and
hatred amused themselves by nailing their prisoners in different postures;
and so great was their number that space could not be found for the
crosses nor crosses for the bodies.[13]

Although this nightmare scenario took place a generation after the crucifixion of Jesus, the possibility of such destruction surely haunted the
minds and hearts of the people of Judea during Jesus' lifetime. The
Romans arrived in Judea and Galilee in 63 B.C.E., and terror and destruction marked their rule from the beginning. Recall that there was an upris-
ing in 4 B.C.E., near the time Jesus was born. Roman retaliation for this
included the burning of Sepphoris, a large town only a few miles from
Nazareth, and the mass enslavement of the population there.[14] Surely
Mary and Joseph knew about this, and were frightened by it. Perhaps they
even knew people who died, or who were enslaved. Suddenly the Gospel
reports that Jesus' family thought him insane make a little more sense. In
a world where any sort of political upheaval can lead to the kind of mass

violence practiced by the Romans, anyone with sense would want to silence someone like Jesus before he got not only himself killed, but God only knows how many others.

In this atmosphere of fear, repression, and despair, Jesus' preaching of the reign of God could be seen as a stunning, life-transforming burst of new hope—or as absolute lunacy. As Monika Hellwig argues, the crowds that initially followed Jesus eventually turned on him because they understood all too well what he was asking of them:

> What the listeners apparently discerned quite correctly was that this was no invitation to repentance that simply called for an acknowledgement of sinfulness and helplessness in the situation while waiting for the salvation of God to come somehow from outside the situation and outside of human freedom. Jesus proclaimed the presence of the Reign of God now, if only they would accept it. In other words he proclaimed that the grace or gift of God was not being promised in the future and withheld in the present but was present empowerment for a totally different kind of life and society. If the empowerment of God is already there, it leaves his listeners with the burden of response, the burden of risk in a radical change of lifestyle and relationships and expectations.
>
> The keynote of all this, as his listeners correctly saw, is vulnerability. To live now as though God alone reigned in human affairs and no sanctions, reprisals or injustices were to be feared, is by all ordinary standards plain foolishness while in fact God does not really reign in human affairs. It is self-interest and greed for wealth and lust for power over others and a desperate unslakable thirst for recognition and status which rule the affairs of human society for the most part, now as then.[15]

The interesting thing here is that those who listened to Jesus and eventually rejected him recognized something that many Christians today have failed to see: this is not about a simple acknowledgment of sinfulness and a passive waiting for God to make it all better. Rather, Jesus' call to repentance was a call to a new way of life—a way of life that could get you killed. Today, that understanding of the radical nature of Jesus' message is often lost on those of us who live safe and relatively comfortable lives in the West. In the Third World, however, many people have realized that their situation mirrors that of the Gospels. If you're living in a military dictatorship where a few powerful people rule over masses of disenfranchised peasants, where friends and family are "disappeared" for no apparent reason, where political dissent brings violent reprisals, suddenly the Gospels read very differently. And Jesus' choices begin to look different, too.

Too often we've spoken of Jesus' death as part of a greater plan, or as simply inevitable, or as his unquestioning, devout obedience to an inexplicable command of God. That dismisses the real situation Jesus was struggling through, and casts God as a monster. Rather, Jesus preached and taught that God's reign exists here and now, and that we should live out that truth in all our relationships: love and compassion should be the ground and flowering of our lives. To preach such a thing, and to live in such a way, is terribly threatening to those who are trying to run the world through fear and intimidation. Jesus was an immense threat to the powers in charge of daily life around him, because he wasn't afraid of them. And if people listened to him, and no one was afraid anymore, then rule by fear and terror was over. But to truly live out what he was preaching, Jesus was called to follow a path marked by twin signposts: ever-increasing love, compassion, and identification with those already crushed by society, combined with the ever-increasing risk that the forces that crushed others would crush him, too. And rather than abandon his mission, rather than abandon the poor he so thoroughly embraced, and the God he so deeply trusted, Jesus kept going along that path until its bitter, brutal end. As Monika Hellwig describes it:

> Jesus enters progressively into the dilemma of the human situation and into the greatest suffering and rejection that the social sin of the human community can inflict upon the unfortunate. Jesus as God's word of compassion enters progressively into those domains of injustice, oppression and evil in which the compassion of God is most needed. . . . Jesus crucified is a naked man among the stripped and unprotected of the world who cannot clothe themselves in the privileges of power. And that is his last word to us. He died as he lived, among the poor and disregarded and unprivileged by his own choice.[16]

And that's why Jesus' death matters to us: because he entered into what Hellwig calls the dilemma of the human situation and what also could be called the very depths of the human situation. He was abandoned by his dearest friends, he was beaten and mocked, he endured horrific pain, and he died as a public spectacle. It doesn't get much worse than that. And if we are still asking why, the answer now is simple. The creator of the universe, God Almighty, chose to enter into human life and human struggle and human pain and despair to the fullest extent possible, that his presence might comfort us always. We are never alone. Jesus has been there; God *is* there with us, always. Jesus was not a hero who escaped what the rest of us go through. He was not far away and untouchable; instead, he was as vulnerable as we are. God's deep compassion for us extended to being with us through torture and death. At no point did he say, "No, sorry, can't go there—I'm too good for that. That's only for lowly beings like yourselves." His humility and suffering love are astounding.

For the past two thousand years, in wildly different cultures all over the world, people have responded to this message. *God is with you.* Even if you are despised, are outcast by your society or religion, are suffering physical pain or mental agony—no matter what, God is with you. The presence of God surrounds you, and loves you. God's great compassion embraces you, including all your mistakes and wrong choices and the stupid, mean things you said yesterday. You are beloved; we are beloved. We are all God's beloved, and live our lives in the embrace of God. Knowing we are loved, we are called to go forth and share that love with others, especially the lost, miserable, and afraid who most need to hear this good news.

A Personal Journey

In my own life, I discovered this powerful association between Jesus' death and God's compassionate presence in my life over the course of several painful years. When I was growing up, I had never understood why they called the day of Jesus' death "Good Friday." What on earth was good about it? The murder of God could not by any stretch of the imagination be called good. I thought it was very strange, but it didn't really have much emotional power for me. Then when I was twenty-one, my mother died, after years of illnesses that had piled up on each other and snowballed into such a tangle of mental and physical pain that she often longed to die. The spring after her death, Good Friday went from being a theologically inexplicable but emotionally irrelevant day to being a day of crushing grief. Now I knew what the disciples had felt in losing someone they loved, and their loss reminded me of my own, and the combination was overwhelming. How on earth did they get from Good Friday to Easter Sunday? I couldn't imagine anyone pulling themselves up out of the depths I was discovering.

I struggled for the next several years with depression—sometimes half-recognized, sometimes ignored—and finally, I couldn't ignore it any longer. My lowest point came one February (never a good month in Minnesota): I felt incredibly alone, completely overwhelmed, and helpless to do anything but sleep as much as possible. I finally decided I needed help when I realized that I was seriously contemplating running away from home—a lunatic idea for a thirty-three-year-old woman with a husband and small child. Run away? It was clear to me that my thinking had regressed to the point where I was approaching the world the way I did as a teenager, when my greatest desire during my parents' divorce was to "run away" and live somewhere else, with anyone else, in order to escape what was happening at home. So I got help: I saw my doctor, started seeing a psychologist, and found a spiritual director. The combination of all these things started pulling me up from the depths—and then there was Holy Week.

I was having a terrible day—couldn't stop crying, hated myself for how weak I was being and what a terrible mother I was, felt miserably alone. And then my pain opened into something new, into a revelation of a truth much larger than anything I was experiencing that day. I was suddenly confronted with the realization that Jesus had been alone, like me—and even more alone. His friends ran away when he was in trouble; mine were actually trying to help, as much as they could, even if I felt that they didn't really understand. Jesus had been exhausted with grief and loneliness and pain. Jesus had been where I was, and so I was not alone. *I was not alone!* What a tremendous revelation! Suddenly Good Friday WAS good. It was the day when Jesus' absolute commitment to me was revealed. Jesus was willing to be with me—with all of us—through the depths. We are never alone. I was amazed, overcome, deeply grateful, and full of awe. I still am. What a gift! "I am here with you, always. I love you."

A Cosmic Truth

Important as it is on an individual level, this tremendous gift of God's presence revealed in Jesus' suffering and death is much more than a personal story. Suffering love is, in the end, the very ground and form of our universe. This is not only a religious or specifically Christian claim; instead, it gives us a story and an interpretation of reality that meshes with and even helps explain the wider functioning of the world. This is a surprising thing to say in our technological and scientific age, but it is true. Let me explain. We live on a planet that is approximately four billion years old, in the midst of a universe that—to the best estimates of physicists today—is about fourteen billion years old. Our universe is stunningly ancient, and grew from nothing to the unimaginable expanse of starlight, space, and life that surrounds us today. God's creation is vast, beautiful, and rather frightening to contemplate, overall. The thought of being only a small planet in an obscure solar system somewhere in one of several billion galaxies punctures any pretensions we might have about being the center of the universe.

The scientific story of where we are and how we got here raises serious questions for Christians. It challenges not only our egos but our ability to believe in a loving God. After all, this is a universe that seems to thrive on destruction, pain, and suffering. For any creature to survive, it must destroy/eat another part of God's creation. Even the very elements that make up human cells were created through destruction: when ancient stars blew up as supernovae, the immense heat and pressure transformed the hydrogen and helium of the star into heavier elements such as carbon, oxygen, and nitrogen—the very stuff of our lives. And then there is evolution: so much waste, so many failed attempts at survival over billions of years. Would a good and loving God—a God who revealed himself as compassion itself—create such a universe, and design it so that life must feed on suffering and death? Why wouldn't a good and loving God create a perfect universe, one in which life did not depend on death, or at least in which suffering was not so staggeringly prominent? Theologian John Haught explains that only when we understand God as suffering, humble love will we understand why the universe has unfolded in such a slow and stumbling manner:

> Since it is the nature of love, even at the human level, to refrain from coercive manipulation of others, we should not expect the world that a generous God calls into being to be instantaneously ordered to perfection. Instead, in the presence of the self-restraint befitting an absolutely self-giving love, the world would unfold by responding to the divine allurement at its own pace and in its own particular way. The universe then would be spontaneously self-creative and self-ordering. And its responsiveness to the possibilities for new being offered to it by God would require time, perhaps immense amounts of it. The notion of an enticing and attracting divine humility, therefore, gives us a reasonable metaphysical explanation of the evolutionary process as this manifests itself to contemporary scientific inquiry.[17]

In the end, knowing that God's creation exists through divine humility and self-emptying love, we are able to see that the entire story of creation is one that unfolds through compassion. Suffering is and must be a very real part of creation as it wends its imperfect, halting way towards God, but it is surrounded and borne up always by the compassionate presence of God, which not only called us into being but calls us ever onward toward God's true life in love. The twin realities of suffering and love intertwine: God's love enables us to live in freedom; our freedom and independence from God mean that mistakes, immaturity, and selfishness are all too real and all too cruel; God's love surrounds us as we struggle through suffering toward the truth of God. At the center of the story is the passion and death of Jesus, revealing definitively that the fundamental nature of reality is self-emptying love and eternal compassionate presence.

The Resurrection Changes Everything

Yet this isn't, as it were, "the end of the story." Jesus' death was not the end of the story; indeed, if the story ended there, it wouldn't have the same meaning at all. Everything that happens in a story transforms the meaning of what has come before; the same story with a different ending is an entirely different story. The best example I know of this is the musical *Jesus Christ Superstar*, which ends with the crucifixion, not the resurrection. *Jesus Christ Superstar* is a story marked throughout by tragedy, grief, and agony—the end of the story works back and infects even the opening with despair. It is the story of Jesus without the resurrection, and so it is not a story of hope and promise for the poor or the lost, but a story in which violence and corrupt power crush our hopes for justice, love, and new life. Its overall effect is, in short, devastating. The beauty and power of the music only drive home how awful, how terrible this story is.

But that story is not ours. The Christian story does not end with the terrible death of Jesus, but with the resurrection. *And the resurrection changes the entire story!* No longer is it a story of a good man destroyed by the powers of the world, nor the story of a failed revolution, nor that of a man whose belief in love was shown to be dangerously naïve. Just as Codi's new knowledge of her family relationships to half the town of Grace enabled her to understand her childhood and indeed her whole life in a new way, so, too, do we understand Jesus in a completely different way once we get to the resurrection. A preacher and healer who died a miserable death is no big surprise and no big news; it happened many times in Israel's past, and is still happening in the world around us. People who stand up for the poor and the outcast often end up poor and outcast themselves, and some of them die, though today they're more likely to be riddled with bullets than hung from a cross. Recent Latin American history is rather full of such cases, from Oscar Romero and the four church-women (Dorothy Kazel, Maura Clarke, Ita Ford, and Jean Donovan) in the 1980s, to the more recent killing of Juan Gerardi Conedera, "auxiliary bishop of Guatemala City, who was beaten to death in April 1998, just two days after releasing a report blaming the military for most of the abuses committed during the country's 36-year civil war, during which 200,000 people died."[18] No, the death of Jesus could have been read as a story we know all too well: it was the resurrection that changed it into a story of hope and power.

Early Christians interpreted the resurrection in two important and powerful ways, and today we have yet another way to understand how the resurrection changes our understanding of the story of Jesus. First of all, early Christians experienced the resurrection as *God's vindication of Jesus*. The manner of Jesus' death could be used to argue that Jesus was a failure, and that everything he said was a lie, but the resurrection showed that God was on his side, to the point of freeing him even from death. Secondly, early Christians interpreted Jesus' resurrection as the *true beginning of the reign of God*—the new age in which (among other things) God would raise the dead. Paul called Jesus the "first fruits" of the general resurrection that would see all the dead arise into a new life in God (1 Cor. 15:20).

But there is one more point to be made about the resurrection, one that we can see especially clearly because we are paying attention to stories. *The resurrection means that Jesus' story is not over*. And if Jesus' story did not end with his death, then it continues even now, in our own lives. As Monika Hellwig points out, the resurrection is not a matter of "hearsay evidence for us, but a matter of direct experience."[19] This is a startling and powerful statement: we are Christians not because we believe someone else's story of the resurrection, but because we have directly experienced, in our own lives, the love and power of this man, Jesus of Nazareth. He lives! We trust what he said so long ago because we know and trust him today. And we are called to journey with him, in love, compassion, and risk, toward our new life in God.

Notes

1. If you're interested, a good place to start an investigation is a study of the Gospels of John and Thomas in Elaine Pagels, *Beyond Belief: The Secret Gospel of Thomas* (New York: Random House, 2003).

2. Elizabeth Johnson, *She Who Is: The Mystery of God in Feminist Theological Discourse* (New York: Crossroad, 1992), 95.

3. Ibid.

4. Ibid., 98.

5. Ibid., 99.

6. Ibid., 87, 89.

7. The literal translation of John's "and lived among us" (1:14) is "pitched his tent among us." The image is clearly one more in tune with a nomadic culture than with our own, but it carries such a wonderful impression of arriving in the middle of our hectic lives and "camping out" just outside our front door.

8. Monika Hellwig, *Jesus, The Compassion of God: New Perspectives on the Tradition of Christianity* (Collegeville, MN: The Liturgical Press, 1992), 75.

9. Ibid., 76–77.

10. For a fuller discussion of Jesus and the purity system, see Marcus J. Borg, *Meeting Jesus Again for the First Time: The Historical Jesus and the Heart of Contemporary Faith* (San Francisco: HarperSanFrancisco, 1994), 49–61.

11. See Bernard Brandon Scott, "Leaven," in *Re-Imagine the World: An Introduction to the Parables of Jesus* (Santa Rosa, CA: Polebridge Press, 2001), 21–34.

12. Richard Horsley, *Jesus and Empire: The Kingdom of God and the New World Disorder* (Minneapolis: Fortress Press, 2003), 27.

13. Josephus, *War of the Judeans*, 5.449-51, quoted in Horsley, *Jesus and Empire*, 29.

14. Horsley, *Jesus and Empire*, 30.

15. Hellwig, *Jesus: The Compassion of God*, 87.

16. Ibid., 94.

17. John Haught, *God After Darwin: A Theology of Evolution* (Boulder, CO: Westview Press, 2000), 53.

18. Paul Jeffrey, "Justice in Guatemala," *Christian Century* (June 20, 2001): 8.

19. Hellwig, *Jesus: The Compassion of God*, 103.

CONCLUSION
Living within the Christian Story

We began with a song—Tom Conry's haunting meditation on Easter and the continuing struggle of the Christian community. "Ancient death is still within us," we sang, but God has begun something new in Christ. And that something new can be seen and shared—in bread, in stories, and in the hope that binds us together:

Though the waves assault the palisades and all creation groan,
In the midst of song and story no life stands alone.
All that pass the cup of passion and the bread that makes us free,
We have watched the water parting and walked dry-shod through the sea.
Bread has gathered us together and the hunger makes us one;
Then let all the earth set seal to what God has now begun.

All who walk upon the water, all who wander on the waves.
They shall see the fury ended, they shall know the One who saves.
They shall hold apart their future from their unrelenting past
Until morning shall have risen and the first become the last.
Songs have gathered us together, and the stories make us one;
Then let all the earth set seal on what God has now begun.[1]

We are creatures of story, beings who create stories in order to create connections—connections in time, in space, and between people. "In the midst of song and story, no life stands alone." We bind ourselves to a particular history and a particular community through the stories in which we choose to live. Make no mistake: we *do* choose the stories within which we live. We are not passive victims of time and circumstance, but protagonists of history, and active participants in the songs and stories that shape us, teach us, and bless or curse us. As Christians, we have chosen to live inside a breathtaking, all-encompassing story: that of God's

155

ongoing relationship with all of creation. Every year, at the Easter Vigil, we remind ourselves of the breadth and depth of this story. The Scripture readings that night begin with the creation of the universe, continue on with God's promise to Abraham, the Exodus, God's ongoing relationship with Israel, and finally, the life and death and blessed resurrection of Jesus. That is our story. It is a tremendous one, a powerful one, and it shapes our lives and our understanding of the world around us.

The Christian story within which we live, however, is not the only story of our lives. Instead, we live in the midst of many interlocking and over-lapping stories. Our own story is built out of the stories that hold together the history, hopes, and meaning of our nation, our hometown, our family, our religion, and our own past. At first glance it might seem that we have little control over this maze of stories within which we live, but that is not quite true. There are many ways to tell and interpret any of the stories that form our lives and hearts. The events of the past are fixed, but we choose how to interpret them, and which ones are key to the story we are telling. This is especially easy to see in debates over how to tell the story of our nation's history: my home state, Minnesota, is currently embroiled in a bitter dispute over setting up social studies standards for elementary and high school students. Should students be required to know more about Ronald Reagan than Franklin Delano Roosevelt? What should they be taught about the war in Vietnam? Was the civil rights movement a minor aside or one of the key events of the twentieth century? Clearly there is plenty to argue about, and it is equally clear that different answers to these and other questions will result in wildly different stories of the truth about our country.

In our own lives, the choices are often just as stark. For example, my mother's long illnesses and eventual death can be the grounds for several different stories: in one, her own poor choices led to their easily antici-pated consequences. In another, misogynistic doctors ignored her com-plaints until it was too late to save her. Then there is the story of a woman of courage and fragility, betrayed by the weaknesses of her body. The vil-lain shifts in each of these stories: my mother herself, the doctors, her body. The lesson shifts, too: "Put your health first, and if the doctors say that worrying is causing your ulcers, *stop worrying*." "You can't trust doc-tors." "Our bodies are not our true selves; we are spirits trapped in decay-ing flesh." Each of these stories is true enough, as far as it goes, and at one point or another, I have embraced all of them. The story I look to most right now is an attempt to put all of these into a wider context; it is a story that emphasizes the reality of human brokenness (things my mother should have and should not have done, choices the doctors might have made instead, an acknowledgment of the utter fragility of human health and life) while insisting that this reality is not what is *finally* true about her or about life. Brokenness, sin, and suffering are all very real, but they are smaller than love. When I tell my mother's story now, the center of it is not how she died but how she loved: the children she raised, the music she played, the laughter she shared. Those are the things that are finally true.

Clearly, our choices and our interpretations shape the stories of our lives. And so we must be especially careful when we commit our lives to the story of Jesus—or rather, to a particular story of Jesus. Living within the Christian story entails a choice about *which* Christian story will rule our hearts, for there are many Christian stories. It is possible to read the story of Jesus as a story of judgment, punishment, and shame, and it is equally possible to see the story as one of compassion and new possibilities. Many of us grew up living in Anselm's version of the story, in which we are wicked servants, despised by God because of our sinfulness but somehow saved anyway. Others find themselves living within the story Calvin told, a story in which justice is harsh and punishment severe. another story with the prime message that we are not worthy to be loved by God. These stories, powerful as they are, engage our fears more than our hopes, and present us with images of God that flatly oppose Jesus' portrayal of his beloved Abba. We need to live within a different story; we need to *choose* another story, and enter into it with our whole hearts.

And we can. Our tradition provides us with several clues about how to tell that story, and so do our own experiences of God's presence, of seeking wholeness, and of the flexibility of time and storytelling. We have Julian's story of the eager servant, in which God does not condemn us for our shame, sins, and faults, but instead seeks to offer us a reward for our struggles, our hurt, our too-often-frustrated attempts to seek what is real. We have Abelard's story of God's love luring us toward an imitation of that love. We have the medieval tradition of the maternity of Jesus, reminding us that Jesus' tender care for us is like that of a mother for an infant. We have the Jewish and Christian traditions of the Wisdom of God, relentlessly calling to us and offering us hope, refreshment, and new life. And, of course, we have Jesus: the stories he told, the stories his friends told about him, and our own stories of our encounters with the Lord of life.

We know, after listening to the stories women tell in *Beloved*, *Animal Dreams*, and *A Weave of Women*, that God's presence is all around us, that the wholeness we seek includes but does not unduly emphasize the suffering we endure, and finally, that the end of the story often changes the meaning of all that went before. We have, in the end, a surprising, profound, and radical story of the truth of compassion, the power of love, and the growing, undeniable reality of the reign of God. When we choose to live within Jesus' story of the reign of God, we enter a whole new life. We are comforted by his presence. We know that suffering was deeply a part of his story, and will certainly be part of our own, but it won't define the story. After all, that story does not end with the crucifixion, and it will not end for us in pain or defeat or death, either (though our stories will include all those things). Instead, our story, like Jesus', includes and is ultimately defined by the resurrection, which is God's resounding affirmation of love and life. The joy of the resurrection renews the whole earth, and certainly renews, centers, and grounds our lives.

In the end, we are Christians because we are living inside Jesus' story of the reign of God. We are part of the story he revealed to us, the story that God has been telling since the beginning of time. When we enter Jesus' story, we become not merely *believers* in his story, but *disciples* of the One who is telling the story. As disciples, we follow the path laid out by Jesus in his life and death and resurrection. To be a disciple is to be not merely a student, passively ingesting information, but to be a traveller, one who follows in someone's path.[2] And that is what we are: travellers, disciples, followers after Jesus. Our life's journey toward him is a journey in and toward compassion and hope. We are journeying with Jesus to the very heart of God.

Notes

1. Tom Conry, "What God Has Now Begun," verses 3 and 5, on *The Fire Within the Night*, compact disc (Portland, OR: OCP Publications, 1994). © 1989 Team Publications. Published by OCP Publications, 5536 Ne Hassalo, Portland, OR 97213. All rights reserved. Used with permission.

2. Marcus J. Borg, *Meeting Jesus Again for the First Time: The Historical Jesus and the Heart of Contemporary Faith* (San Francisco: HarperSanFrancisco, 1994), 135.

INDEX